BENJAMIN FRANKLIN

BENJAMIN FRANKLIN

THE NEW AMERICAN

by MILTON MELTZER

Franklin Watts
New York / London / Toronto
Sydney / 1988

Photographs courtesy of: Library of Congress:
frontis, p. 191; Culver Pictures: pp. 17, 23,
58, 91, 93, 97, 103, 229, 251; New York Public
Library Picture Collection: pp. 28, 37, 68, 75, 89,
100, 115, 126, 151, 176, 180, 183, 189, 217, 240,
272; Bettmann Archive: pp. 33, 63, 73, 129, 206, 231,
237, 254, 259; Historical Society of Pennsylvania:
pp. 124, 163; Benjamin Franklin Papers, Yale
University Library: pp. 136 (top), 168; Beineke
Library, Yale University: p. 136 (bottom);
Metropolitan Museum of Art: p. 203.

Library of Congress Cataloging-in-Publication Data

Meltzer, Milton, 1915-
Benjamin Franklin: the new American / Milton Meltzer.
p.   cm.
Bibliography: p.
Includes index.
Summary: Presents a biography of the multi-talented and
accomplished founding father.
ISBN 0-531-10582-2
1. Franklin, Benjamin, 1706-1790—Juvenile literature.
2. Statesmen—United States—Biography—Juvenile literature.
3. Printers—United States—Biography—Juvenile literature.
[1. Franklin, Benjamin, 1706-1790. 2. Statesmen.]   I. Title.
E302.6.F8M5 1988
973.3'092'4—dc19
[B]
[92]   88-17015   CIP   AC

For Pat, Jessica and Alex

ALSO BY MILTON MELTZER

George Washington and the Birth of Our Nation

The American Revolutionaries:
A History in Their Own Words 1750–1800

The Landscape of Memory

Mark Twain: A Writer's Life

Dorothea Lange: Life Through the Camera

Betty Friedan: A Voice for Women's Rights

Winnie Mandela: The Soul of South Africa

Mary McLeod Bethune: Voice of Black Hope

Ain't Gonna Study War No More:
The Story of America's Peace-Seekers

Never to Forget: The Jews of the Holocaust

Rescue: The Story of How Gentiles
Saved Jews During the Holocaust

All Times, All Peoples:
A World History of Slavery

The Black Americans:
A History in Their Own Words

The Jewish Americans:
A History in Their Own Words

Langston Hughes: A Biography

A Pictorial History of Black Americans
(with Langston Hughes and C. Eric Lincoln)

CONTENTS

BENJAMIN FRANKLIN

INTRODUCTION

Why do we smile when we hear the name of Benjamin Franklin? No other name among the Founding Fathers is as familiar to everyone growing up in America. Yet his name does not inspire awe. No, we start calling him "Ben" almost from the moment we meet him on the printed page or see his face in the myriad images that have come down to us. We feel we could be comfortable with him at our table as we never could with the aristocratic George Washington, the intellectual Thomas Jefferson, or the starchy John Adams. He seems to be the most agreeable of persons in the international Hall of Fame.

Perhaps we feel at home with him because, like most of us, he started life with few advantages. Yet, though born a tradesman, he became the most celebrated man of his time. No other man of his generation—and perhaps since—has been as multi-talented and accomplished. He is the self-made man, the first American to set the pattern that innumerable others have tried to follow. Many of them achieved wealth or political power. But Franklin did more. He proved to be an astonishing success at whatever he turned his hand and mind to: printer, publisher, businessman, author, general, inventor, scientist, politician, diplomat, philosopher, and more. Yet, in whatever he did, wherever he was, he always remained himself.

His reputation, wrote John Adams some time after Franklin's death, "was more universal than that of Leibnitz or Newton, Frederick or Voltaire, and his character more beloved and esteemed than any or all of them. . . . His name was familiar to government and people, to kings and courtiers, nobility, clergy and philosophers, as well as plebeians, to such a degree that there was scarcely a peasant or a citizen, coachman or footman, a lady's chambermaid or a scullion in a kitchen who was not familiar with it, and who did not consider him as a friend to human kind."

His name, his ideas, his leadership are linked to the creation of the Declaration of Independence, the success of the American Revolution, and the writing of the United States Constitution. From his *Autobiography*, his letters and other writings, and the findings of many students of the man and his times, we shape this portrait of Benjamin Franklin.

CHAPTER ONE

BOSTON BOYHOOD

It is almost three hundred years since Benjamin Franklin was born in Boston. (The date was January 17, 1706.) It is hard to put yourself back in that time and grasp what it was like. About 12,000 people lived in Boston, and in all the English colonies of North America there were only 250,000. (That's about the same as the population of Rochester, New York, today.) Most of the people were clustered around Boston, the Connecticut and Hudson river valleys, eastern Virginia and Maryland, and Charleston, Carolina. They had little connection with one another. Roads were really paths, and bad weather made them almost impassable. People traveled little except by sea. Surrounding the settlements were hostile Indians who made travel almost as dangerous as did the primitive roads and bridges. With the country so thinly settled and communication so difficult, it was easier to stay in touch with England than with the neighboring colonies.

Ben was born into a large family. He was the fifteenth of seventeen children his father Josiah had by two wives. Families of such size were not only common then but were also a great economic asset. Fertile land was cheap and labor scarce. All but the very young children were set to useful work on a farm or in a trade. In the towns, boys worked in their father's shop at a very young age, doing the simplest chores. Son after son renewed the labor supply. As they left for apprenticeships elsewhere, the younger brothers took their places. The young girls helped run the home, learning the skills needed to feed and clothe the family and keep the house clean and warm. Daughter after daughter gave aid to terribly overworked mothers who were pregnant much of the time. And soon the girls, usually quite young, left home to marry and start large families of their own. Rarely did more than half of such large families reach adult life. But in Josiah's family thirteen grew up "to settle in the world," Ben said.

If the average life span was brief, the number of births was so high that Americans rapidly filled up the eastern parts of the colonies and by Ben's time began to move west across the mountains.

Of the seventeen children ten were male, and Ben was the youngest of them. Much later, when his insatiable curiosity led him to dig into family history, he discovered he was the youngest son of the youngest son for five generations. His father Josiah had migrated from England in 1683, bring-

House where Franklin was born,
on Milk Street in Boston

ing his wife and three children. When Ben traced family records, he was pleased to learn his ancestors were all plain people: farmers, blacksmiths, dyers. Hardworking, but not enterprising, none of them made a mark in the world. Josiah himself had been an apprentice dyer in the home country, and now in Boston was a maker of candles and soap. From his shop came the candles the Boston watchmen carried to light up the night. His trade did well; when Ben was six, his father was able to move family and shop into a new house cornered at Union and Hanover streets. Over the door hung the sign of his trade, a big blue ball. This was the center of town, close by the wharf, where ships loaded cargoes for far-off ports.

Ben would grow into a man with many of his father's characteristics. Strong, energetic, independent, a "mechanical genius" handy in the use of other tradesmen's tools. "His great excellence," Ben wrote of his father, "lay in a sound understanding and solid judgement in prudential matters, both in private and public affairs." Often a dozen or more people sat around the family table—family, friends, neighbors—with Josiah starting a conversation on some "useful topic" his children would enjoy and profit by.

Josiah had five healthy children by his first wife, Anne. But the sixth child died within five days, and eighteen months later, Anne died a week after bearing a son, who himself died within a few days. At a time when death happened daily, the Puritans spent no time brooding over it. Josiah buried wife and child and went back to the problems of living. He was thirty-one now. His trade had to be carried on, the house maintained, the meals cooked, the clothing made. He found a new woman, twenty-two-year-old Abiah Folger, and married her five months after Anne's death.

She was a fine choice, for the Folgers had a zest for life, a great curiosity about the world, and a desire to make it better that enriched the line of Franklins. Abiah was the daughter of Peter Folger, who helped settle Martha's Vineyard and later its neighboring island, Nantucket. Like so many men of his time, Peter Folger mastered several trades. He was a teacher, surveyor, miller, weaver, and interpreter for and defender of the Indians. Abiah's mother Mary had been an indentured servant her father bought and then married. Although Ben says little about Abiah, we know he thought her "discreet and virtuous." Prolific too, she bore Josiah ten children in twenty-two years, and all healthy, like herself and Josiah. (She died at eighty-four, he at eighty-seven.) In all those years she must have had little time for anything but childbearing and chores.

Small as Ben's Boston seems to us now, back in his childhood it was the largest town and the busiest port in North America. The twisting streets were paved with cobblestones, gutters ran down the middle, geese honked on the Common, and pigs were the roving garbage collectors. Tiny timbered tenements forced the crowded Bostonians into outdoor living whenever the weather permitted. Only the rich knew comfort and privacy in their red brick mansions fringing the Common. Their wealth came from trade with the West Indies and from shipbuilding. The young Ben soon realized that trade was the way to prosperity and power. He saw that men who started as carpenters and shoemakers could end up on Beacon Hill if they made their way into shipbuilding or commerce.

As plentiful as the great forests that made shipbuilding a major industry were the raw materials for what became the largest iron industry in the world. Milling products and rum too were important colonial enterprises. Early on, the merchants of New England, New York, and Pennsylvania did good business with Europe and the West Indies. A pattern of triangular trade grew up. It was based on the large consumer markets and the cheap manufactured products of Europe, and the needs of the flourishing plantations on the sugar islands. Central to it was the shipment of cheap rum from New England to Africa to be exchanged for slaves. This human cargo was then transported to the West Indies and sold for gold, bills of credit, and molasses. The gold and bills of credit went to England to pay for manufactured goods, while the molasses ended in New England distilleries, where it was converted into rum. And that began the cycle once again.

We think of Ben Franklin as one of the first modern men. Yet it was only ten years before he was born that the witchcraft mania ended. The English colonists of the 1600s lived in a world of fear and superstition that bred belief in demons,

witches, and evil spirits. Few people knew what
caused such natural events as floods and earthquakes and lightning. In New England, ignorance
and repression nourished a witchcraft hysteria that
brought the execution of twenty people at Salem
in 1692. Yet at the same time the work of such
pioneer scientists as Copernicus, Galileo, Kepler,
and Newton was penetrating European minds and
uprooting ancient beliefs. Slowly the new science
crossed the Atlantic. What it was based on—confidence in the power of human reason, or rational-
ism, as it was called—began to shake old religious
faith. A liberal wing of Protestantism took hold. It
stressed morality, not piety. And as prosperity
spread in the colonies, a secular view of the world
crept in.

By the early 1700s, Boston was becoming a place
where contrasting points of view could be heard.
The new century into which Ben was born was
open to new ideas and new values. And even a
whisper of freedom might be heard, not only from
the authoritarian church around the corner but
from the Crown far off across the sea.

Back in England, Franklin after Franklin had
gone into the blacksmith shop. What other choice
did they have? Only privileged people could own
land, enter a profession, or hold office. If you were
not born that lucky, life was hard: your fate was
fixed. It was why Josiah left for America. A dissenter, he wanted religious freedom as well as economic security. True, he found the privileged ran

Boston too, but by the late 1600s their grip on power was no longer so tight. Josiah carried on in his work, respecting what he did and knowing his own worth. He trained two sons in his trade and lost a third who went to sea and drowned.

Josiah raised his children to be pious. The family went to the Old South, the Congregational Church. There were books at home, most of them on religion, and Ben learned to read. He says he didn't know how he learned to read; he just did. He was a promising boy. At seven Ben wrote some verses he asked his father to send in a letter to an uncle in London. That uncle—another Benjamin—delighted in the child's scribbles and encouraged him to go on with his pen. A little praise is often all it takes. It marked the beginning of Ben's long life as a writer—among many other things.

It was at seven, too, that Ben had another experience he often recalled. One holiday he was given a little money to spend on whatever he liked. He headed straight for a toy shop but on the way met a boy blowing a whistle. Charmed by the sound, he gave him all his money for it. Coming home, he whistled piercingly all over the small house, annoying his family. When he told them of the bargain he had made, they teased him for paying four times what the silly whistle was worth. He realized how many good things he could have bought for the money, and while they laughed, he cried. It was a lesson he never forgot. Often, when he observed people squandering money or time or

*Young Ben upsetting the family
with his costly whistle*

health or energy on something foolish or worthless,
he would think, "They give too much for their
whistles."

It was now that Josiah decided he would have
Ben prepared for a career in the church. After all,
he was the tenth of his male children, and this
would be a proper tithing of his progeny. There
was no more important calling in Puritan Boston.
Parents believed it was the highest and best use to
which a son's talents could be put. Ben had shown

so early a readiness to read and study that Josiah could do no better for him than point the way to the ministry and the doing of public good.

To become a preacher required schooling: six years at the Latin School and at least four at Harvard College. At Harvard, founded seventy-eight years earlier, six out of ten students became ministers. Although it was the acclaimed profession, it did not bring a comfortable living. That, Josiah did not mind. So Ben, now eight, was told what his future would be and was launched on his formal education.

Public education open to all children was very uncommon in the colonies. Only Massachusetts and Connecticut required every town of fifty or more people to support a public school, a law that was usually ignored. Most children were educated at home. Few families could afford anything more than a bit of training in reading, writing, and arithmetic. As for going beyond that, besides Harvard there were only two other colleges: William and Mary in Virginia, and Yale in Connecticut.

The Boston Latin School had been founded just five years after the town was settled and was supported by public funds. Ben was one of a hundred pupils. Most of the boys in his beginning class were his age. The course of schooling was keyed to Harvard's entrance requirements: you had to be able to use Latin as the language of all instruction and to be familiar with the classical Greek authors in the original language. Ben proved he had a gift for learning, sailing to the top of his class by the middle of the year. He was told he would skip a grade the next year. But before that could happen, Josiah decided to take him out of the Latin School—and to give up the idea of preparing Ben for the ministry. Later Ben wrote that his father's reason was the expense of an education. That seems unlikely. Tuition was free at the Latin School, and at Harvard promising boys were given scholarships and jobs as waiters to cover other expenses.

The real reason, probably, was that though Ben was bright enough, he was not pious enough to be a minister. Josiah had evidence of that. Ben had found his father's painfully long saying of grace before and after meals simply too tiresome. One day after the winter's provisions had been salted, young Ben spoke up at table: "I think, Father, if you were to say Grace over the whole cask—once for all—it would be a vast saving of time."

In a town where the longer a religious exercise was, the more virtuous, the point was not lost on Josiah. A shrewd man, he understood that his son didn't care much for theology or the pulpit. Ben was no doubt mightily relieved that he would be spared a career in the church. Neither by temperament nor by conviction was he fitted for it. Josiah switched him to a more practical training and sent him to one of Boston's many schools for writing and arithmetic. Girls too went to such schools; they could not go to the Latin School or to Harvard.

Most of the men in Boston were literate in this period, and about three out of five of the women.

George Brownell's school was just two blocks away from home. The main stress was on learning to write a good clear hand. Less attention was paid to the art of composition. Apart from the talk, the written word was then the only means of communication. Whether you were to be a scholar or a tradesman, you had to master writing. Ben did well in it, but poorly in arithmetic. Enough, his father said. And that ended Ben's formal schooling.

But if Ben went to school for only two years, he never ended his education. By studying on his own, he would become one of the best informed and most learned men of his century. All life long he devoured books. But what books? His insatiable hunger is the more remarkable when we think how limited was the range of reading offered a boy in his time. There were almost no children's books, no novels, no stories written for boys. But Boston was a bookish town: the written word counted for much in the Puritan mind. Private citizens built up their own libraries. They were often rich in the classics as well as in science, medicine, and natural history. Even Josiah, the hardworking soap- and candle-maker, had a home library, small but varied enough for Ben to feast in it. True, his father's shelves had some of the dullest arguments over theology ever printed. The boy read them anyhow, unable to resist anything in print. Perhaps it was here that he began to feel that religious controversy was wasteful and pointless. His religious belief was simple: "Serving God is doing good to man."

Josiah's shelves offered better food for the mind. First, there was John Bunyan's stirring story of *The Pilgrim's Progress*. Ben was so pleased with it that when a little money came his way, the first thing he bought was a set of Bunyan's works in cheap little volumes. Published only a generation earlier, *The Pilgrim's Progress* had been written in prison by a simple thinker turned preacher. The prose was lean, spirited, inventive. Bunyan was the first English writer to use dialogue in telling a story, a method Ben found engaging because it made the reader feel that he was sharing directly in the life of the characters. The adventurous plot, the graphic scenes, the convincing characters with their mixture of weakness and strength, failure and success, rushed Ben along from page to page. Strong as the story was, even more impressive to Ben was Bunyan's view of life. Progress—man could make progress, that was Bunyan's belief. Christian, his hero, resolutely makes his way through one obstacle after another. Progress, Ben came to believe, was not a gift from Heaven. He could shape a goal for himself, and advance toward it, armed by faith in himself and in the power of the mind. This would be the core of his life, the power behind his rise.

After Bunyan, what captured Ben was Plutarch's *Parallel Lives of the Noble Greeks and Romans*. Plutarch, a Greek who lived in the first century A.D.,

Feasting on books

was the pioneer biographer. He wrote forty-six biographies in pairs, one Greek's life compared to one Roman's life. Though proud of his Greek culture, Plutarch was fair and honest in his portraits of the Romans. A superb craftsman, he made the *Lives* juicy reading, exciting to all ages and especially to young people like Ben. Plutarch's stories demonstrated that the boy is father to the man by using rich anecdotes to make his point. His stories were thick with adventure, such as Pompey's chasing of the pirates out of the Mediterranean, a story that was very real to Ben, who had seen pirates executed in Boston. This was personal history, told through the experiences of great men. And again, as in Bunyan (though here are real, not imagined lives), Ben saw people driving toward productive goals. Plutarch honored men who lived useful lives, while portraying the evil of men doing only harm or spending their lives idly. And all this done with such charm and verve that Plutarch is still read everywhere two thousand years later.

For a boy with such little schooling, Burton's books were another find. R. Burton was really Nathaniel Crouch, once a printer's apprentice in London, who wrote a batch of little books that sold for twelve pennies each. They were crisp rehashes of material on great events and strong personalities, or on "oddities, rarities and wonders." Full of information on everything from earthquakes to famous women, they fed Ben's eager appetite for facts and broadened his view of the world beyond Boston.

The ideal of progress was stamped upon Ben's mind by Bunyan and Plutarch. But what brought it down to earth for him was the writing of another man, the journalist Daniel Defoe. At this time Defoe had not yet produced his famous popular novels, *Robinson Crusoe* and *Moll Flanders*. It was an earlier work, *An Essay on Projects*, that fell into Ben's hands. Defoe was a dissenter, both in religion and in politics. Like Franklin, he thought the kingdom of God on earth was best advanced by men and women behaving decently and fairly with one another. Defoe looked around his England and saw many social and economic ills, for which he prescribed some cures. If people used their power to reason, he said, they would remove obstacles to reform and save the victims of injustice. Defoe, like the mature Franklin, was able to see problems clearly and then find a workable way to correct them. In his *Essay* he took up dozens of social problems and projected a method to solve them or at least alleviate them. His book proposed medical insurance against losses and fires, cooperatives to help widows, pensions for merchant seamen and the aged, medical aid for the sick and disabled, regulations for banking and the stock market, commissions to improve highways, and more. And in a male-dominated age, he attacked the unjust treatment of women, calling for the opening of academies to educate young women to the fullest extent of their capacities and interests.

Of course Ben was not allowed to sit in a corner and do nothing but read. Like everyone else in the family, he was put to work.

CHAPTER TWO

PRINTER'S APPRENTICE

There was only one path open to Ben. Since he had turned away from the ministry, then he must, like most Boston boys, master a craft to provide him with lifetime security. So Josiah made his youngest and last son an apprentice in his own trade. Now going on sixty, Josiah could give Ben the benefit of his long experience and the prospect of owning a solidly established business. I'd rather go to sea, Ben said. But one son had already vanished into the ocean mists, and Josiah wouldn't have it.

Apprenticeship was a traditional stage in growing up. The custom went back to the Middle Ages. The usual term in England was seven years, ending somewhere between the ages of twenty-one and twenty-four. In England guilds of craftsmen set the regulations for apprenticeship, but there were no guilds in the colonies. They failed to take root here because America was largely agricultural and because of the great distances between settlements and the shortage of skilled labor. Here anyone could call himself a master craftsman and take on apprentices.

Not all craftsmen were equal, and Josiah Franklin's trade placed him at the bottom. To be ranked at the top among craftsmen meant your earning power was greatest. And that in turn depended upon how hard or easy it was to become a master craftsman. It took little time or skill to become a candle-maker—but a lot more to become a silversmith. And, too, that trade required fine tools and expensive raw materials.

It turned out to be a sad decision forced upon Ben. In Josiah's trade there was no room for Ben's inquiring and inventive mind to operate. Making soap and candles was honest and useful work, yes, but it was also stinking, dreary, boring work. The soap and candles were made from tallow rendered from beef and mutton fat. The long process took some skill but needed nothing from Ben's brain or talents. Josiah and Ben had to work twelve to fourteen hours a day and six days a week to meet their orders and make a living. Ben boiled the soap, cut wicks for the candles, fitted the molds for cast candles, attended the customers, and ran errands. He hated it and didn't mind letting his father know it.

What time was left after work, Ben spent exploring the port of Boston. He hung around the wharves, observed the teeming life in the marshes, watched the men at work in the shipyards and

*The apprentice candlemaker pours
tallow into the molds.*

ropewalks, listened to the tales of the seamen. He learned early to swim expertly, developing powerful arms and shoulders. He loved playing in the water and showed how inventive he could be at his favorite sport of swimming. Not content with using his hands and feet to swim, he made oval paddles to be held in the palms, with a hole for the thumb, and increased his speed. Then he added flippers to be fastened to his feet to further increase his speed. He even figured out how to use a kite while in the water. He lay on his back, holding a stick in his hand with the kite string attached to it, and let the wind sweep the kite through the sky and propel him across the pond.

With his self-assurance he was the boy the others turned to when in difficulty. Sometimes he led them into scrapes. He organized the neighborhood gang into building a wharf out over a millpond so they could fish from it instead of standing in the mud. They took the stones from a large heap intended for a new house near the pond. At night when the workmen had gone home, the boys came out to lug the stones to the pond where they made their little wharf. The theft was soon detected, and their fathers "corrected" them. Though Ben argued how public-spirited his idea was, Josiah convinced him that "what was not honest could not be truly useful."

Two years passed. Josiah came to accept the fact that another trade must be found for this strong and willful son. Though he was obedient at home, he could be unpredictable. Josiah feared that Ben might run off to sea if he were forced to stay in the shop. So he wisely began walking with Ben through the town, showing him the many other trades. Together they watched bricklayers, millers, cobblers, carpenters, roofers, joiners, braziers, turners, coopers, millwrights, shipwrights, leather workers, metal workers, all doing their job. Nothing throughout his life pleased Ben more than to see a good craftsman making something or to feel the right tool for a job in his own hands.

Still no decision. At last Josiah turned to his own family for help, a well-established custom. His nephew, Samuel Franklin, had come over from London to take up the trade of making cutlery, repairing and selling knives. Samuel's aging father, Benjamin the Elder, had been living for four years, free of charge for his food and lodging, in Josiah's home. Ben went into Samuel's shop, but when only a few days had passed, Samuel said he wanted to be paid a fee to teach Ben the trade. Josiah must have been furious. In England a fee was customary, but not in America. And this, after he had been taking care of Samuel's father all those years? He told Ben to come home at once.

Then what about printing? Surely it would appeal to a boy so devoted to the printed word. And there was already one printer in the family, Ben's half-brother, James. Ten years older than Ben, James had gone to England to learn the trade and bring home a press and types to set up shop in Boston. This was much better than candles and soap. Ben, now twelve, signed an indenture to serve James as an apprentice. Indentures were a standard agreement, requiring the master to provide the apprentice with his meals, clothes, a place to live, and to teach him the craft. In return, the apprentice was to work loyally for his master, do whatever he asked, live where told to, and remain with him till the age of twenty-one.

Ben entered James's small print shop quite happily, even though he knew it would be drudgery for some time. He did the usual chores: swept the office and shop, got up early to build a fire, fetched water, ran errands. James did all sorts of job work, including small editions of pamphlets for the book-sellers who also functioned as publishers. He had three competitors in Boston; it was a struggle to hunt up new business. He printed with a wooden press developed by a Dutchman a hundred years earlier, a press that would not be outmoded until the iron press was introduced two centuries later.

When James let him begin, Ben learned to set type from handwritten copy and then moved on to master the use of the wooden press, a complex and exhausting job. He found printing hard work—and slow work. But dull? Never. He was always producing something different. Printing took so many stages to the final publication that Ben and James had to work a twelve-hour day and often two or three hours beyond that. You had to be strong for this labor, but Ben's natural sturdiness was made all the tougher by the swimming he had

Working in brother
James's printshop

done for many years. He couldn't remember ever being so tired after a long day's work that he was unable to read for hours at night.

Boston was full of clever apprentices. Everyone learned a trade that way, and so it had been in Europe and America for many generations. Like Ben, they all wore leather aprons and often leather breeches too. The long hours they put in seem cruel to us today, but they were normal then. Still, the boys had energy enough left over to get into all kinds of trouble. As the historian Esther Forbes tells it, some apprentices behaved like this:

> They lied, seduced their master's daughters, fell through the ice and drowned. They left careless fires and burned down bakeshops or overheated tar in the caboose of a ship and burned up the ship. They stole great wigs and silver spoons. They ran away and were whipped publicly and privately. . . . It seems to have been the ambition of every apprentice to harass the master as much as possible without getting flogged for it. But there was little teaching without a whip in those days. However hard the system sometimes was on boys and masters, the art, craft, mystery, or trade was well served. No other method has turned out such good workmen.

Quickly Ben made himself as expert as his brother and very useful to him. Printing was a craft he never tired of. Whether he was living in America or England or France, he would always have a press at hand. Great as his accomplishments were, when he wrote his last will, he began it: "I, Benjamin Franklin of Philadelphia, printer . . ."

The shop was now quite busy, but Ben made time to go on with his reading—early in the morning, before work, late at night after work, and on Sundays alone in the printing shop. He found ways to get his hands on more books. He talked booksellers' apprentices into smuggling books for him out of their masters' shops at night, stayed up all hours to read them, and returned them early the next day before they would be missed. One of James's customers and friends was a merchant who took a liking to Ben and let him borrow books from his own large library. Stimulated by what he read, Ben tried his hand at writing verse. James encouraged him, and the boy wrote a ballad about the recent sensational drowning of a family in Boston harbor and another about the famous pirate, Blackbeard, who had just been captured and killed off the Carolina coast. James rushed them to press and sent Ben out on the streets to hawk them. This stuff was news the public cared about; it was dramatic and emotional, and was conveyed in pleasing rhyme and meter. The ballads sold well, and the boy's vanity swelled—until his father told him they were rotten stuff and that "verse makers were generally beggars; so I escaped being a poet," Ben said later, "most probably a very bad one."

Writing prose was different. In that he became superbly skilled. The talent was "a principal means of my advancement," he said. It proved of great use all through his life. How he mastered writing at so young an age is a remarkable story. One of his Boston friends was another "bookish" boy, John Collins. The two friends enjoyed arguments. For the fun of it they would take opposite sides of an issue such as women's right to an education and debate it to develop their skills. Ben thought John a more eloquent speaker, who beat him more for his fluency than for the strength of his reasoning. One day Ben sat down to write out his argument, and John replied on paper. They exchanged a few such letters when Josiah happened to find them and read them. Without commenting on the merits of the debate, he told Ben that he could spell and punctuate decently, but his use of language fell far short of what it should be.

Instead of being crushed by his father, Ben was determined to improve his style. A London paper, *The Spectator*, was very popular in America at the time. It was written by two men, Joseph Addison and Richard Steele, highly praised masters of English. Ben got hold of a volume of *The Spectator* and read the witty and satirical essays over and over. He was delighted with them. He set about making a few notes on one of the essays, then put them away for a few days before trying to write on the theme in his own words and manner, as best he could. When finished, he would compare his version with the original, discover his faults, and strive to correct them. He would also turn some *Spectator* essays into verse, then back again into prose, enlarging hs vocabulary and polishing his style. He got up early in the morning and stayed up late at night to practice writing. His drive for excellence was unlimited.

Ashamed of his ignorance of arithmetic, he found a book on the subject and mastered it. From a book on navigation he studied the fundamentals of geometry. Then he read the Englishman John Locke's *Essay Concerning Human Understanding*. Published thirty years earlier, it was a monumental work that powerfully influenced eighteenth-century thought. Locke was by nature a moderate man, a man who sought to conciliate differences. In a spirit of tolerance he tried to compromise clashing views without giving up principle. If political authority was legitimate and just, he opposed revolution. But where a government was tyrannical, he advocated effective protest.

Ben was captivated by the book's brilliance. It shaped his own ideas and strengthened the values he would live by. Locke was open to the new, to change in an ever-changing world. To dismiss something just because it was new was foolish, he said:

Truth scarce ever yet carried it by vote anywhere at its first appearance: new opinions are always suspected, and usually op-

posed, without any reason but because they
are not already common. But truth, like gold,
is not the less so for being newly brought
out of the mine.

Locke did not pretend to divine authority the way
the Puritan preachers of Boston did. His style of
talking with his readers rather than lecturing them
made it easy to follow his argument. The result
was to enlarge Ben's understanding of everything
Locke discussed—science, religion, politics, education, ethics, philosophy. Perhaps there were limits
to what the human mind could know, but, Locke
said, "Our business here is not to know all things,
but those which concern our conduct."

To be doubtful, to be skeptical, was not a bad
thing. The mind, man's power of reasoning, "must
be our last judge and guide in everything." Young
Ben, still groping for a place to stand, found firmer
footing as he read and reread Locke. These were
ideas in which he could believe and by which he
could live.

Earlier Ben had found humanitarian principles
in one of Cotton Mather's works, *An Essay Upon the
Good*. Many of Mather's flood of publications were
dull, boring, impenetrable. But not this book. The
Puritan minister, whose family had dominated Boston for generations, thought that good things done
in this life prepared the way for the next. Ben had
never been concerned with the hereafter. But
Mather's lively interest in the world around him

was evidence of a generous devotion to the welfare of the people of Boston. He thought about the community, wanted his "brethren to dwell together in unity, and carry on every good design with united endeavors."

Ben had the same sense of community and would demonstrate it a thousand times over in the years ahead. He liked to be with others, men and women, to share work and pleasures and ideas with them. The welfare and progress of whatever community he lived in was of great importance to him. Cotton Mather was at the top of Boston's social ladder, and Ben the apprentice was at the bottom. Still, when Mather wrote this, Ben knew it was meant for him:

> My friend, thou are one that makes but a little figure in the world, and a brother of low degree; behold, a vast encouragement! A little man may do a great deal of hurt. And then, why may not a little man do a great deal of good! It is possible the wisdom of a poor man may start a proposal that may save a city, serve a nation! A single hair applied unto a flyer [a flywheel] that has other wheels depending on it, may pull up an oak, or pull down a house.

One day Ben came across a book that contained examples of some fifty dialogues of Socrates, the philosopher of ancient Greece. Because Ben had

not gotten very far in his debates with his friend
Collins, he was eager to learn about the Socratic
method. He was "charmed" by what he read, by
the calm temper of Socrates, by his lack of aggres-
siveness, by the moderate way he talked. He saw
that head-on collisions with people who differed
from him were not useful. They thought him
obnoxious and stopped listening. Much better to
be modest and tactful in expressing an opinion.
The Socratic method of asking leading questions,
rather than making self-serving assertions, was
effective way back then and always would be. It was
far more likely to lead to the truth.

In 1721, when Ben was fifteen, his brother
decided to publish a newspaper, the *New England
Courant*. Colonial printers had begun to combine
job printing—that is, the printing of religious tracts,
schoolbooks, laws, almanacs, and sometimes even
literary works—with bookselling and the publication of newspapers. Boston already had two such
papers, both put out by printers who were also
postmasters and thus were able to have the post-
riders carry their papers free. That privilege naturally made them careful not to offend authorities
who could remove their privilege. James's would
be the first independent newspaper in the colonies.

Bostonians had little light reading to enjoy at
the time. The two existing newpapers served the
stuffy establishment by publishing official orders
and proclamations. Fresh news or ideas found no
place in their pages. Poets and essayists, budding

politicians or social reformers had no outlet for their feelings. James saw his opening and launched the *Courant*. It was but a single sheet, printed on both sides.

No editor had an easy time gathering news when communications were so poor. What was happening in Europe mattered much to Americans. But sailing vessels took months to bring the news from abroad. There was no cable, no radio, no telephone, no television, no computer electronics to speed the news from here to there. When news did break into print, everyone knew it was old and stale. James would do better: he would at least entertain Boston by publishing satirical commentary on local events and personalities. And like some news media of today, he would create exciting news when he couldn't find any. He did that by working up sensational controversies to stir reader interest.

Ben's was a modest role at first. He set the type for the *Courant* and printed off the sheets. Then he carried the paper to the customers, a few hundred at most. James gathered around him several young "wits" to write pieces and provoke controversy. James himself wrote some essays and doggerel verse. Excited by the stir the paper was making, Ben wanted to try his hand at this new journalism. Perhaps he saw his pen as the means to free himself of always being looked down upon as merely a boy and an apprentice. He loved the written word, and he was learning much from books. Why not assert himself in print? Tell the community what he believed and describe what he had observed? And, maybe, do something to improve life in Boston?

James still saw him as a boy. Ben knew his brother would object to printing anything he wrote. So, taking up one of the many pen names he would use throughout life, he tried his hand at the familiar essay, the literary form he had studied in *The Spectator*. He wrote a piece of his own and at night slipped it under the print shop door. James found it the next morning, liked it, and published it. This was the first of a series of essays by "Mrs. Silence Dogood," a busybody of a widow with a saucy pen. She was a delicious change from what Bostonians were used to. Ben put his own thoughts into her mouth and sprinkled her speech with generous quotations from Defoe and Cicero. Mrs. Dogood made fun of religious hypocrites, the town drunks, and women's hoop petticoats. She argued for freedom of speech, proposed insurance for widows and spinsters, and asked why girls shouldn't be educated as much as boys.

The Dogood essays were rooted in *The Spectator* and in Defoe. But the material—Silence Dogood herself and the other characters, the events, the talk, the attitudes—they were Boston to the bone. From the age of ten, when he began delivering candles for his father, to now, Ben had acquired a deep familiarity with almost every aspect of local life. His pieces made Boston laugh at itself, gave it a fresh slant on its fads and follies, let it see what attitudes were outworn and what changes were needed. All were done with a lightness and humor that were ingrained in Ben and would always mark his writing.

After fourteen Dogoods, Ben ran dry and stopped. Now he told James who Dogood really was. Instead of being pleased by Ben's talent, James was annoyed. This upstart brother of his was getting too big for his britches. After all, *he*, James, was still the master, and Ben still the apprentice, and he expected the same obedient service from Ben due any master. Ben didn't like it: shouldn't a big brother be more lenient? But James was a passionate man, Ben said, "and had often beat me." That tyrannical treatment gave Ben a hatred for arbitrary power that stuck to him for life. When, how, would he get rid of this apprenticeship?

Meanwhile, the *Courant* was plunged into a controversy over inoculations against smallpox. Just as the paper began to appear, Boston suffered an appalling outbreak of smallpox. Within months it killed one out of every ten citizens. For six hundred years it had terrified Europe. By Shakespeare's time it was by far the greatest cause of death. Millions died of it, and many millions more were blinded or crippled by it. The lucky survivors were pockmarked for life. Boston had already suffered five devastating attacks. Although the clergy believed it was God's will, others thought something should be done at least to reduce its terrible effects.

A fierce debate raged over how best to fight it. Isolation of the sick was the old method; it helped but did not stop the epidemic. But what about the new approach, inoculation? Cotton Mather, the Puritan minister long interested in science and medicine, had heard from his slave, Onesimus, that inoculation was practiced successfully in his African homeland. Matter was taken from the pustules of a person with a mild case of smallpox and inserted into the bloodstream of a healthy person through small incisions. The result was usually a light case of the disease that produced long-term immunity. Other Boston slaves confirmed what Onesimus had said. Mather learned that it had worked well in Constantinople, too. From his pulpit he urged it upon Boston as the only way to halt the scourge, and most of the clergy supported him. Medicine was medieval then, and only one doctor, Zabdiel Boylston, endorsed the idea. He successfully inoculated Mather's son, his own son, and a slave, and then others desperate to try anything. His was the first trial of immunology in the Western Hemisphere.

Immunization against smallpox had never before been used in Boston or in Britain. Mather could not guarantee it would work for everyone or even for most. But what other choice was there? James Franklin and his *Courant* contributors refused to believe that Cotton Mather had the way out of this horror. Mather's role in the Salem witch trials had ruined his reputation for them. Besides, the very idea of preventing a disease by causing it seemed to most people—as it did to almost all the physicians—wildly illogical. No one knew then about disease-causing microorganisms.

One of James's friends, Dr. William Douglass, took the lead in attacking Mather violently in the *Courant* and ridiculing inoculations as quackery. The town was so frantic that someone flung a fire bomb into Mather's house. Luckily, it fizzled out. Mather was furious at the *Courant's* blind resistance to the only way to save human life. James wouldn't listen; he detested Mather, and he was out to sell papers. But Mather was right and was very brave to champion inoculation against such harsh abuse.

Altogether, Dr. Boylston inoculated 242 people; only six of them died. That was a death rate of 2.5 percent. But the death rate for the thousands of Bostonians who contracted the disease naturally was 14.6 percent. Dr. Boylston's account of the epidemic in Boston and his inoculation trials was published in London and earned him membership in the Royal Society.

In his *Autobiography*, written long after, Ben never mentions the smallpox controversy of 1721. The reason will become clear later.

At last the epidemic petered out, but not the *Courant's* ridicule of Mather, the clergy, or the colony's royal governor, Samuel Shute. Shute was eager to censor anything in print he disliked. But James, while he was learning the printer's trade in London, had seen how freely the English press wrote about public issues. Now he stoutly defended the freedom of his own paper to print what its writers thought.

Shute was fed up with the *Courant*'s hive of bees buzzing in his ears and stinging him whenever they liked. He seized the opportunity to punish James when the editor charged in the *Courant* that the governor had dillydallied in pursuing pirates menacing the coast. For this "scandalous libel" he threw James in jail for a month without a trial. Young Ben took over, editing and publishing the next issue by himself. Barely seventeen, he was the youngest editor in America. Three weeks later James was released and went right on putting out a lively and independent paper, critical of Boston's political and religious authorities.

The next time the *Courant* offended, in 1723, the general court forbade James to publish the *Courant* (or any other paper or pamphlet) unless everything in it was first approved by the secretary of the province. It was an appalling order, amounting to prior censorship of anything James wanted to print. The British Parliament had revoked that power nearly thirty years earlier. Governor Shute didn't care.

But the ban was on James himself, not on anyone else. To get around the order, James made Ben the nominal publisher of the paper. To avoid the charge that Ben was really an apprentice acting under his master's orders, James signed papers officially discharging the boy from his indenture.

But he had Ben secretly sign another indenture to keep his services for the remainder of his term. The *Courant* appeared under Ben's name for several more months. Then the brothers had another quarrel. Ben decided this was the time to win his freedom, for he knew James wouldn't dare to reveal the secret indenture.

Seeing that his young brother meant to leave, James tried to keep him from getting work elsewhere in Boston by telling the other printers not to hire him. It didn't stop Ben. "I was too saucy and provoking," he said later, and although he knew it was unfair to take advantage of James, he was seventeen now and wanted badly to be out in the world on his own. Defying his brother, as well as his father—who said he had no right to leave James—and the ruling powers of Boston, who had already labeled him an atheist and a radical, he ran away.

CHAPTER THREE

PHILADELPHIA AND LONDON

The nearest place to get work as a printer was in New York. Ben sold some books to raise passage and boarded a sloop sailing south. In three days he was in New York, hundreds of miles from home; he wrote, "a boy of but 17, without the least recommendation to or knowledge of any person in the place, and with very little money in my pocket." He asked an old printer, William Bradford, for a job. I need no help, Bradford said, but my son Andrew in Philadelphia might be able to offer you work in his print shop.

Philadelphia was a hundred miles away. Ben set out by boat, and after a storm at sea, a fever, a long hike, and an overnight row in another boat, he reached Philadelphia at eight o'clock on a Sunday morning. His arrival is a classic passage in his *Autobiography*:

I was in my working dress, my best clothes being to come round by sea. I was dirty from my journey; my pockets were stuffed out with shirts and stockings; I knew no soul, nor where to look for lodging. Fatigued with walking, rowing, and want of sleep, I was very hungry, and my whole stock consisted of a Dutch dollar and about a shilling in copper coin, which I gave to the boatmen for my passage. . . .

I walked towards the top of the street, gazing about till near Market Street, where I met a boy with bread. I have often made a meal of dry bread, and inquiring where he had bought it, I went immediately to the baker's he directed me to. I asked for biscuit, meanings such as we had in Boston, but that sort it seems, was not made in Philadelphia. I then asked for a threepenny loaf and was told they had none such. I told him to give me threepennyworth of any sort. He gave me accordingly three great puffy rolls. I was surprised at the quantity but took it, and having no room in my pockets, walked off with a roll under each arm and eating the other. Thus I went up Market Street as far as Fourth Street, passing by the door of Mr. Read, my future wife's father, when she, standing at the door, saw me, and thought I made—as I certainly did—a most awkward, ridiculous appearance.

Ben met a young Quaker on the street who directed him to a lodging house. In the morning he went to Andrew Bradford's print shop only to find

another hand had just been taken on. Bradford
sent him to a new shop run by Samuel Keimer.
This man impressed Ben as only a novice, with a
battered press, worn-out types, and no skill at
presswork. Still, it was a job, and he took it. Keimer
sent Ben next door to Mr. Read's for lodging.
Cleaned up and better dressed, he looked more
respectable now to Read's daughter, Deborah.

Philadelphia was scarcely fifty years old in 1723.
Founded and planned by the English Quaker William Penn, it had already grown nearly as big as
Boston. Ben soon learned it was a far freer community than his birthplace. Penn had provided for
toleration of all religions, for free education, for
the election of representatives, and for jury trial in
open court. He made it easy for poor immigrants
to buy land and pay for it in installments. It was
an asylum for the persecuted and a happy place
for craftsmen, traders, shopkeepers, and home-
steaders. With energy and an enterprising spirit,
thrifty young men like Ben Franklin could make
something of themselves in this "City of Brotherly
Love." By the time Ben arrived, the early English
settlers had been joined by waves of Germans,
Welsh, Scots, and Irish. The port was the principal
gateway to the British colonies.

Walking along the waterfront, Ben could see
scores of merchant ships crowding the Delaware,
waiting to load or unload at twenty wharves. Horses
and furs, tobacco and lumber, grain and beef went
off to the other colonies, to the West Indies, or to

Britain, and a great variety of manufactured goods, together with rum and molasses, entered the port. People too were a steady import, with many immigrants settling in the town and many others passing through, taking the wagon road across the mountains to reach the western lands or heading south for Virginia and the Carolinas. Rich in natural products, Pennsylvania was now adding to its prosperity by making iron, textiles, and ships.

The Quakers, though only a fraction of the population, were by far the best-off citizens. Yet the Friends, as they were called, had not abandoned their beliefs to achieve success. Many clung to the habits of plain living (some did not), hard work, and thriftiness. Their faith did not interfere with making good in business. (They were just as industrious as the Puritans.) Nor did it bar them from taking part in politics. They collected libraries and encouraged science, providing a cultural setting that would nourish the keen mind of young Franklin.

Ben found it a very congenial town, even though the Quakers tried to control public conduct by barring theaters, sports, and gambling. The people amused themselves in clubs and taverns. The streets were unpaved and poorly lit, and disease plagued the town.

Ben thought Samuel Keimer was an odd fish to work for—slovenly, rude, a little knavish, but still a thinking man. In Ben's time with him, Keimer reprinted a British publication called *The Indepen-*

dent Whig and sold it weekly for a penny. It was the first periodical other than a newspaper to see print in the colonies. Keimer liked it for its dissenting view of religion. It also advanced the idea of political independence, an idea that took root in the colonies.

You could not yet call Pennsylvania a true democracy. The heirs of William Penn, known as the "proprietors," were often away in England. Together with the local bigwigs—the merchants and landowners—they dominated politics. The council did their bidding.

Ben made young friends who shared his interest in reading. By living frugally, he managed to save some money. He rarely thought about Boston and kept his whereabouts secret until a brother-in-law, captain of a sloop, learned where he was and wrote him that the family would forgive and forget and welcome him home. Ben replied that he had nothing to be forgiven for. Sir William Keith, governor of the province, saw the letter and dropped in on Ben at the shop. Keith, an odd and unreliable man, liked the young printer and proposed that if Josiah would set Ben up in a shop, the governor would hand him the colony's printing business, as well as Delaware's.

Ben sailed up to Boston to try his father out. The family was glad to see him again. But Keith's proposal? No, said Josiah flatly; Keith must be a fool to think of setting up an eighteen-year-old boy in a man's business. Josiah would not lay out the considerable sum required. Ben did not seem very upset. He went over to his brother's shop to strut, showing off his new suit of clothes, a watch, and pockets jingling with silver. James "looked me all over, and turned to his work again." Ben chatted with the journeymen, showed them his watch and silver as James looked on. Then he tossed them some coins to buy themselves a drink. James was furious. He would never forgive or forget that insulting behavior.

Josiah told Ben to go back to Philadelphia, behave respectfully, avoid getting into political scrapes, work hard, and if you earn enough by the time you're twenty-one, I'll help set you up in your own print shop. So Ben sailed back to Philadelphia, this time with his parents' blessing. When Sir William heard that Josiah would not do it, he promised to set up Ben himself. He told Ben to prepare an inventory of what he'd need as a printer and to go to London to buy it with Sir William's letters of credit and introductions to influential friends. You may repay me when you are able, he said. Ben was so flattered by this attention that he never doubted his word. No one had told him that the governor very easily made promises that he never meant to keep. Now he seemed the most generous man in the world.

At that time only one ship a year sailed between Philadelphia and London, and it would be some months before it would leave. Ben continued working for Keimer. And, living in her father's house,

*Ben courts Debby Read;
both were eighteen.*

he began to court Deborah Read. "I had great respect and affection for her, and had some reason to believe she had the same for me." He was thinking of marriage, but her mother said that since both Ben and Debby were only eighteen, it would be wiser to wait till Ben's return from England.

Meanwhile, Ben was often invited to the governor's house and was reassured that the important letters of credit would be aboard ship when he left for England. When the time came, he said good-

bye to his friends and "exchanged promises" with
Deborah. On November 5, 1724, when the *London
Hope* sailed, Ben was aboard but not the vital letters.
His hopes for printing equipment of his own
collapsed. What would he do in London without
connections, a job, money for passage home? He
found comfort in a friend who had joined him in
steerage. James Ralph, a merchant's clerk, was a
lover of books, a good talker, and a scribbler of
verse. Ralph, though married and having one child,
went along on the voyage, he said, to try to establish
connections abroad.

Landing in London after a three-month voyage,
Ben and Ralph found lodgings together. Ralph
now confessed that he would never go back to
America. He had deserted his wife and child,
throwing them on her relations' hands. Nor did he
have a penny after paying his passage. He began
to borrow from Ben while looking for work. Ben
found work at once at Palmer's, a large printing
house, and then at Watts's, an even bigger one that
employed nearly fifty printers.

Here he amazed his beer-guzzling shopmates
by drinking water. Some of them drank five pints
of beer a day, before, during, and after work,
boasting it gave them strength. The young "water-
American," as they called him, showed he was able
to carry a large form of type in each hand up and
down stairs while they could carry only one with
both hands. Ben had turned vegetarian while ap-
prenticing for his brother in Boston. Plain living

had appealed to him, and besides, the less money spent on meat and drink, the more he had for books. In London he observed how the outlay for "the cursed beverage," beer, kept the workers in poverty.

He preferred to spend much of his earnings on the pleasures of London—plays, music, books, treating his unemployed friend. A nearby dealer in secondhand books let Ben borrow them for a small fee. Ben wrote and printed a skeptical little pamphlet he later regretted. When it came into the hands of a Dr. Lyons, a surgeon and himself an author, it brought him a new friend who took him to alehouses and introduced him to good company and good conversations.

Although still in his teens and a young workman no one had ever heard of, with no achievements to his credit, he had a startling amount of self-confidence. After meeting Dr. Henry Pemberton, a scholar, through the printing house, he asked to be introduced to Pemberton's friend, Sir Isaac Newton, the great scientist, but the meeting never took place. He did manage to be invited to the home of Sir Hans Sloane, a distinguished physician and botanist, and president of the Royal Society; he showed Ben his collection of specimens, and to add to his curiosities Ben sold him a purse that he had brought from America made out of a newly found material, asbestos.

Out to have a good time, Ben seemed to forget his engagement to Deborah. He wrote her only one letter during his eighteen months in London, and that was to let her know he wasn't likely to return soon. This, he said long after, was one of the great mistakes of his life, "which I should wish to correct if I were to live it over again." In fact, he couldn't have returned early because he was spending so much money that he had none for the passage home.

Meanwhile, Ralph had begun an affair with a young milliner he met in their lodging house. They moved in together, but unable to support her and her child, he left town to teach school in a village. With Ralph gone, Ben tried to make love to his friend's mistress, but she turned him down angrily and wrote about it to Ralph. That caused a break between the friends, and Ralph got even by forgetting his debts to Ben. Later Ben said that while his morals at this time were fairly good, his unruly sexual appetite often led him into "foolish intrigues with low women."

The elderly widow he lodged with was of a different kind. A clergyman's daughter, she had known many people of accomplishment. She entertained and educated Ben with innumerable stories about the great. They enjoyed each other's company so much he often spent evenings in conversation with her. When a shortage of cash made him think of finding cheaper lodgings, she reduced his board to thirty-seven cents a week.

Never considered a handsome man, Ben had the charm and wit, the cheerfulness and respect

for others that enabled him to make friends everywhere. His talent for telling stories in a delightful
way would always make him welcome, in print shop
or palace. His workmates at Watts's printing house
could ignore his strange taste for water and enjoy
his company. He taught his friends there how to
swim and went with them on boating trips. Once
he stripped, leaped from their boat on the Thames,
and swam the four miles from Chelsea to Black-
friars, displaying all the feats, under and on water,
that he had mastered back home. One friend at
Watts's proposed that he and Ben tour Europe
together, paying their way by their trade.

But now, after eighteen months in London, Ben
grew homesick. Thomas Denham, a Quaker merchant he had met on the voyage to England, took
a liking to him and asked him to return to Philadelphia with him, where he proposed to open a
store. He wanted Ben to assist him and promised
quick advancement and eventually a better living
than a compositor could earn.

So Ben quit printing—forever, he thought—
and in July 1726 sailed for Philadelphia with Denham. The voyage home took nearly three months.
He kept a journal while at sea, and in it recorded
the incidents of the voyage in great detail, omitting
much of this in the *Autobiography* he wrote long
after. Some of the twenty-one passengers played
cards. When one of them was caught cheating, the
others agreed to ostracize him. Ben thought this

Earliest known portrait of Franklin,
painted about 1746 by Robert Feke

the worst of punishments because man is such a sociable being.

He noted the beauty of dolphins circling the ship, the whipping of a steward for some mild offense, and when they hailed a ship from Dublin bound for New York with fifty indentured servants aboard, he recorded their misery and what a "lousy stinking rabble" they had been turned into by the terrible conditions on board. Again and again, he observed wind and weather, the passengers' shifting moods, the seaweed and the crabs scuttling over it. Nothing was too insignificant to escape his eye. When he wrote of a flying fish, it was with the same fine detail that Thoreau would display in his *Journal* more than a hundred years later.

Not these things, but a plan for regulating his future conduct was what Ben considered the most important part of his journal. Those pages have disappeared, but a fragment remains that shows how he meant to live. Up to this point—he was twenty—he had had no design in mind. Life had been "a confused variety of different scenes." Now he would set out a plan that would help him live more rationally: he would be truthful, sincere in every word and action. He would be industrious in whatever he did, not letting himself be diverted by foolish plans for getting rich quick. And he would speak no ill of anyone, only the good he knew of them. He believed he stuck to this code "pretty faithfully," right through to old age.

It was October 11, 1726, when his ship landed
at Philadelphia. Denham opened a store and took
Ben on as his clerk. Only three months later, the
merchant sickened and died. His living gone, Ben
returned to his old trade—printing.

CHAPTER FOUR

PRINTER, PUBLISHER—
AND HUSBAND

Ben swallowed his pride and went back to work for the old printer, Samuel Keimer. From Ben's description of him in the *Autobiography*, Keimer comes off badly. But it was Keimer who advocated teaching blacks to read long before Franklin had thought of it. And now, despite Ben's running off to England, he gave him the job he needed so badly and paid him high wages.

Ben was to be foreman of the print shop, a business Keimer ran badly, using raw, cheap labor. Cocky Ben said he quickly taught the four workers their trade and got the business in good shape. When the shop ran short of types, Ben fashioned the molds they needed and cast the types in lead. He also made the ink and the engravings and, in short, he said, was "quite a factotum."

But as the other workers improved, Ben became less necessary, and Keimer tried to cut his wages. They quarreled, and Ben walked out on him after six months on the job. With him he took Hugh

Meredith, an "honest and sensible" Welshman, but often drunk. Hugh's father set them up in a printing partnership, providing the capital for it while Ben put in his energy and expertise. Meredith could rarely stay sober long enough to do his part, but Ben tolerated it. He shrewdly fashioned a public image designed to bring in business and establish credit. "I took care not only to be in *reality* industrious and frugal, but to avoid all *appearances* of the contrary. I dressed plain and was seen at no places of idle diversion. I never went out fishing or shooting; a book indeed sometimes debauched me from my work, but that was seldom, snug, and gave no scandal; and to show that I was not above my business, I sometimes brought home the paper I purchased at the stores, through the streets on a wheelbarrow."

That's a hardworking young man, the town said, and since he paid promptly for what he needed, the merchants were glad to do business with him. But no one in those days got rich quick in the printing trade. Most printers had to keep stationery or general stores and go into journalism to make ends meet. Ben decided he would start a newspaper. But when the news leaked out, Keimer beat him to it by launching a paper of his own, the *Pennsylvania Gazette*.

Disgusted, Ben thought he could hurt Keimer by building up the circulation of the rival paper, William Bradford's *Mercury*. He began to write amusing letters for it, signing them "Busy Body."

Numb. XL.

THE
Pennſylvania GAZETTE.

Containing the freſheſt Advices Foreign and Domeſtick.

From Thurſday, September 25. to Thurſday, October 2. 1729.

THE Pennſylvania Gazette *being now to be carry'd on by other Hands, the Reader may expect ſome Account of the Method we deſign to proceed in.*

Upon a View of Chambers's *great Dictionaries, from whence were taken the Materials of the Univerſal Inſtructor in all Arts and Sciences, which uſually made the Firſt Part of this Paper, we find that beſides their containing many Things abſtruſe or inſignificant to us, it will probably be fifty Years before the Whole can be gone thro' in this Manner of Publication. There are likewiſe in thoſe Books continual References from Things under one Letter of the Alphabet to thoſe under another, which relate to the ſame Subject, and are neceſſary to explain and compleat it ; theſe taken in their Turn may perhaps be Ten Years diſtant ; and ſince it is likely that they who deſire to acquaint themſelves with any particular Art or Science, would gladly have the whole before them in a much leſs Time, we believe our Readers will not think ſuch a Method of communicating Knowledge to be a proper One.*

However, tho' we do not intend to continue the Publication of thoſe Dictionaries in a regular Alphabetical Method, as has hitherto been done ; yet as ſeveral Things exhibited from them in the Courſe of theſe Papers, have been entertaining to ſuch of the Curious, who never had and cannot have the Advantage of good Libraries ; and as there are many Things ſtill behind, which being in this Manner made generally known, may perhaps become of conſiderable Uſe, by giving ſuch Hints to the excellent natural Genius's of our Country, as may contribute either to the Improvement of our preſent Manufactures, or towards the Invention of new Ones ; we propoſe from Time to Time to communicate ſuch particular Parts as appear to be of the moſt general Conſequence.

As to the Religious Courtſhip, *Part of which has been retal'd to the Publick in theſe Papers, the Reader may be inform'd, that the whole Book will probably in a little Time be printed and bound up by it ſelf ; and thoſe who approve of it, will doubtleſs be better pleas'd to have it entire, than in this broken interrupted Manner.*

There are many who have long deſired to ſee a good News-Paper in Pennſylvania ; *and we hope thoſe Gentlemen who are able, will contribute towards the making This ſuch. We ask* Aſſiſtance, *becauſe we are fully ſenſible, that to publiſh a good News-Paper is not ſo eaſy an Undertaking as many People imagine it to be. The Author of a Gazette (in the Opinion of the Learned) ought to be qualified with an extenſive Acquaintance with Languages, a great Eaſineſs and Command of Writing and Relating Things cleanly and intelligibly, and in few Words ; he ſhould be able to ſpeak of War both by Land and Sea ; be well acquainted with Geography, with the Hiſtory of the Time, with the ſeveral Intereſts of Princes, and States, the Secrets of Courts, and the Manners and Cuſtoms of all Nations. Men thus accompliſh'd are very rare in this remote Part of the World ; and it would be well if the Writer of theſe Papers could make up among his Friends what is wanting in himſelf.*

Upon the Whole, we may aſſure the Publick, that as far as the Encouragement we meet with will enable us, no Care and Pains ſhall be omitted, that may make the Pennſylvania Gazette *as agreeable and uſeful an Entertainment as the Nature of the Thing will allow.*

The Following is the laſt Meſſage ſent by his Excellency Governour Burnet, to the Houſe of Repreſentatives in Boſton.

Gentlemen of the Houſe of Repreſentatives,

IT is not with ſo vain a Hope as to convince you, that I take the Trouble to anſwer your Meſſages, but, if poſſible, to open the Eyes of the deluded People whom you repreſent, and whom you are at ſo much Pains to keep in Ignorance of the true State of their Affairs. I need not go further for an undeniable Proof of this Endeavour to blind them, than your ordering the Letter of Meſſieurs Wilks and Belcher of the 7th of June laſt to your Speaker to be publiſhed. This Letter is ſaid (in Page 1 of your Votes) to incloſe a Copy of the Report of the Committee of His Majeſty's Privy Council, with His Majeſty's Approbation and Order thereon in Council ; Yet theſe Gentlemen had at the ſame time the unparallell'd Preſumption to write to the Speaker in this Manner ; You'll obſerve by the Concluſion, when it is propoſed to be the Conſequence of your not complying with His Majeſty's Inſtructions (the whole Matter to be laid

---

Front page of the first issue of the newspaper Franklin and Meredith took over in 1729

Unlike his "Silence Dogood" pieces, these did not attack authority or criticize the clergy. Philadelphia must have seemed a better place to Ben than Boston. "Busy Body" simply laughed at oddities in human behavior and offered sensible advice to the readers. While *Mercury* sales went up, *Gazette* subscriptions ran down. In nine months Keimer went broke, sold his paper to Franklin and Meredith, and left for Barbados.

Still, the two young men found it hard going. They did everything themselves, unable even to employ a boy to help them. When Meredith's father ran into financial trouble, he could no longer lend them what they needed. Two friends of Ben's stepped in and offered to inject some capital if he would drop Meredith and carry on business alone. This he did, apparently without a quarrel, and paid off his debts. By 1729 he owned his press, his newspaper, and a shop selling supplies of many kinds: paper, parchment, slates, ink, pencils, quills, maps, legal forms, soap (his father's), lampblack, tea, coffee, lottery tickets, goosefeathers, liquors, groceries, ballads—and books. At the time there was no bookseller's shop south of Boston in the colonies. Devoted readers had to send to London for books.

Ben advertised what he had to sell in his *Gazette*, but ask for anything else and he would manage to get it for you if he saw a chance to profit by it. His newspaper reflected the common practice of trading in people. Such advertisements as these for the unexpired time of indentured servants appeared in his *Gazette*:

> To be sold. A likely servant woman, having three years and a half to serve. She is a good spinner.

> To be sold. A likely servant lad, about 15 years of age, and has 6 years to serve.

> To be sold. A young servant Welsh woman, having one year and a half to serve, and is fit for town or country service. Enquire of the printer.

Other ads dealt with slaves, sold for others or bought by him as an investment.

> A likely Negro wench, who is a good cook and can wash well is to be disposed of. Enquire of the printer thereof.

> To be sold, a likely young Negro fellow, about 26 years of age, suitable for any farming or plantation business, having been long accustomed to it and has had the smallpox. Enquire of the printer thereof.

> To be sold. A likely Negro woman, with a man-child, fit for town or country business. Enquire of the printer thereof.

> To be sold. A lusty young Negro woman, fit

for country business, she has had the smallpox and measles. Enquire of the printer
thereof.

To be sold. A prime able young Negro man,
fit for laborious work, in town or country,
that has had the smallpox. As also a middle-
aged Negro and that has likewise had the
smallpox. Enquire of the printer hereof: or
otherwise they will be exposed to sale by
public vendue, on Saturday the 11th of April
next, at 12 o'clock, at the Indian-king, in
Market Street.

As his biographer Carl Van Doren sizes him up,
"In business Franklin was extremely alert to the
main chance, adaptable, resolute, crafty though not
petty, and ruthless on occasion." For a young man
a practical aspect of getting on in business was to
take a wife with a dowry. From our vantage point
it would seem Ben was a likely prospect for any
young woman in town. He was hardworking, honest, intelligent, tall, sturdy, and if not exactly handsome, not unattractive either. But the parents of
eligible young women did not rush to his doorstep.
He was just a beginner in business, after all, and
that not a very profitable one. He still had debts to
pay, and who knew what his future would be? He
made moves toward one young woman after another. Nothing happened. He began to think his
only chance to get money along with a wife was to

find a woman no one else wanted. For both sexes, love and looks counted, but at that time marriage was primarily an economic undertaking.

Another reason for Ben to seek a wife was his fear of his sexual appetite. In London it had pushed him into affairs with young women he met on the street. Everyone knew how common venereal disease was, disease for which there were then no cures. He dreaded the risk to his health, though luckily he had so far escaped infection. A little older and wiser now, he felt the time had come to settle down.

So he turned his attention once more to Deborah Read. She, despairing of Ben after his long silence in London, had been urged by her friends to forget him and marry another. She did: John Rogers, an able potter but a bad husband. There were rumors too that he was a bigamist, with another wife in London. He spent her dowry rapidly, never made her happy, and shortly disappeared.

Despite Ben's poor treatment of Deborah, her family remained friendly. Ben began to court her again, and their affection revived. Deborah was in a bad way; her husband was gone, but was their marriage legal if he had another wife? And was she a widow or not? Some said Rogers had died; no one knew for sure.

There was a way out: a common-law marriage. She came to live in Ben's house and began calling herself "Mrs. Franklin." It was an arrangement none questioned. Ben "took her to wife" on Sep-

Deborah Franklin. Portrait
by Benjamin Wilson, 1766

tember 1, 1730. He was twenty-four years old. "She proved a good and faithful helpmate," he wrote; "we throve together, and have ever mutually endeavored to make each other happy."

Deborah was a good mate. If she did not bring him a fortune, she helped make him one. He described their household:

> It was lucky for me that I had one as much disposed to industry and frugality as myself. She assisted me cheerfully in my business, folding and stitching pamphlets, tending shop, purchasing old linen rags for papermakers, etc. etc. We kept no idle servant, our table was plain and simple, our furniture of the cheapest. For instance, my breakfast was for a long time bread and milk (no tea), and I ate it out of a twopenny earthen porringer, with a pewter spoon."

Another aspect of that marriage deserves attention. At the time they married, a baby was on the way, or had just been born. (The child's birthdate is given only as c. 1731.) But we don't know whose baby it was. It could have been theirs, conceived somewhat early and now said to be Ben's by an unidentified mother. This to protect Deborah's reputation. Or it could really have been Ben's child by some other woman. At any rate, William Franklin, as he was named, was openly accepted and treated as a son, and became part of the family. So was Deborah's widowed mother, who made and sold in Ben's shop ointments "to remove the most inveterate itch and render the skin clear and smooth."

Debby, as Ben called her, had neither the intellect nor the talents of her husband. Like most women of her time, she was poorly educated; her letters, while informative, affectionate, and often delightful, show her to be almost illiterate. She shared Ben's industriousness and managed their business very well during his many long absences.

THE Widow READ, removed from the upper End of Highftreet to the *New Printing-Office* near the Market, continues to make and fell her well-known Ointment for the ITCH, with which fhe has cured abundance of People in and about this City for many Years paft, It is always effectual for that purpofe, and never fails to perform the Cure fpeedily. It alfo kills or drives away all Sorts of Lice in once or twice ufing. It has no offenfive Smell, but rather a pleafant one ; and may be ufed without the leaft Apprehenfion of Danger, even to a fucking Infant, being perfectly innocent and fafe. Price 2 *s*. a Gallypot containing an Ounce ; which is fufficient to remove the moft inveterate Itch, and render the Skin clear and fmooth.

She alfo continues to make and fell her excellent *Family Salve* or Ointment, for Burns or Scalds, (Price 1 *s*. an Ounce) and feveral other Sorts of Ointments and Salves as ufual.

At the fame Place may be had *Lockyer's Pills*, at 3 *d*. a Pill.

The Widow Read,
Franklin's mother-in-law,
advertises her cure for the itch.

Later, nearing forty, an age when some men become restless in marriage, he sang her praises in a loving poem read in her honor at a club meeting:

Of their Chloes and Phylisses poets may prate,
   I sing my plain country Joan,
These twelve years my wife, still the joy of my life;
   Blest day that I made her my own. . . .
Not a word of her face, or her shape, or her eyes
   Or of flames or of darts you shall hear;
Tho' I beauty admire 'tis virtue I prize,
   That fades not in seventy years. . . .
Am I loaded with care, she takes off a large share,
   That the burden ne'er makes me to reel;
Does good fortune arrive, the joy of my wife
   Quite doubles the pleasure I feel. . . .
Some faults have we all, and so has my Joan,
   But then they're exceedingly small;
And now I'm grown used to them, so like my own,
   I scarce can see them at all. . . .
Were the fairest young princess, with million in purse
   To be had in exchange for my Joan,
She could not be a better wife, mought be a worse,
   So I'd stick to my Joggy alone
                    My dear friends
   I'd cling to my lovely ould Joan.

Two years after his marriage, Ben had paid off all his debts. With the *Gazette*, the print shop, and the store, he was prospering. But as a printer, he worked with his hands. In the eyes of gentlemen, he was only a mechanic. Still, as his reputation rose, the "best" people in town began to invite him, but not Debby, to their homes. That kind of entertaining he did not return. The Franklins lived over their shop, comfortably but modestly. There was always a welcome and a good family meal for those who chose to come by.

Ben's *Gazette* went in more for news than controversy. He had learned from James's experience in Boston not to criticize politicians or the clergy. He covered local events so much better than his rivals that they often stole from his paper, and he teased them for it. He reported epidemics, natural disasters, fires, accidents, and thefts, murders, and rapes in as much detail as modern tabloids. Publishers in those days did not print editorials. A printer was not supposed to have a mind of his own. Instead they tried to shape public opinion by essays of the kind the gifted Ben wrote easily and signed by names like Homespun or Alice Addertongue. The touch was light, the subject local. His eye was on profits, not propaganda. His town, like all of them, was split into political factions. He had to serve all the diverse interests because no one group could assure him of a living. So he was carefully impartial. My goal, he told his readers, is to make the *Pennsylvania Gazette* "as agreeable and useful an entertainment as the nature of the thing will allow." As the *Gazette* proved its profitability, Ben set up his apprentices or journeymen to do business in other places, usually in partnership with him.

Nevertheless, careful as he was, he was often

reproved for printing things critics said ought not
to be published. He replied to them in the *Gazette*
by pointing out that people's opinions were as
various as their faces. Printing has to do chiefly
with opinion, he said. Most things published tend
to promote some opinions or oppose others. Maybe
editors are unlucky to be in a business that can't
avoid pleasing some readers while angering others.
And most important, he said:

> Printers are educated in the belief that when
> men differ in opinion both sides ought
> equally to have the advantage of being heard
> by the public; and that when truth and error
> have fair play, the former is always an over-
> match for the latter.

He himself refused to print personal attacks that
he thought were becoming disgracefully common.
He did not want to injure anyone, no matter who
urged him to or offered to pay him for it. He
concluded that though he despaired of pleasing
everyone, "I shall continue my business. I shall not
burn my press or melt my letters."

Ben's *Gazette* developed into the best paper in
the colonies. Besides the news and advertisements,
he ran essays from *The Spectator*, poems, anecdotes,
a question-and-answer column, and jokes, bawdy
and ribald, typical of the eighteenth-century humor
that appealed to everyone. The *Gazette* looked
nothing like today's newspapers. It was a single

sheet that appeared twice a week. Folded once, it was about 12 by 18 inches. Ben was not an innovator in journalism. He was simply better at what all the other papers tried to do.

The business of Ben's printing press became more profitable as he landed new accounts. He became the official printer for Pennsylvania, and soon after for Delaware and New Jersey as well. That meant printing the state documents, laws, treaties, and paper money for those colonies.

Although Boston led the way for bookselling in colonial times, Philadelphia began to rival it. The town's best-known book dealer was Ben Franklin. His shop offered a wide range of titles on many subjects. By this time book collectors were building notable private libraries. Cotton Mather's collection had nearly four thousand titles, and so did the library of William Byrd II in Virginia. In Ben's colony, James Logan had acquired almost as many books, specializing in the sciences. Earlier, most books were imported from England. To satisfy the growing demand, several printers began to publish as well as to sell books. The largest house in the colonies was Isaiah Thomas's of Worcester, Massachusetts, with about a thousand titles carrying his imprint. Ben's was next, with some eight hundred. He began with two small books of American poetry, and then the first medical book by an American. Ben's press (despite his slave-owning and dealing) brought out two of the earliest antislavery pamphlets, written by the Quakers Ralph Sandiford and Benjamin Lay. To Ben's credit is the first novel to be published in America, Samuel Richardson's *Pamela*. He also put out the first Latin work to be translated (by the same James Logan) and printed in America. When George Whitefield, the great preacher, started a religious revival in the colonies, Ben became his close friend and published his sermons and journals with great success.

The colonial printers, through their newspapers and pamphlets, helped prepare the way for the American Revolution. They heightened the love of liberty and clarified the rights of man so that Americans would be ready, when the time came, to fight for independence and to build their own democracy.

Ben was living in a city whose intellectual vitality could not be equaled elsewhere in the colonies. His own inquiring mind led him to seek out young men of the same spirit. The year after he returned from London—he was twenty-three then—he formed a club for "mutual improvement" that they called the Junto. They met Friday evenings for sociable discussion. The first members, limited to twelve, were mostly young workers. Like Ben himself, they loved reading and wanted to better themselves. In the Junto they could educate one another, making up for the academy or college none could afford. Their members included printers, clerks, a self-taught mathematician, a surveyor, a joiner, a silversmith, a glazier, a shoemaker, and they were soon popularly known as the Leather-Apron Club.

At every meeting each member in turn raised a question for discussion—on politics, morality, history, travel, poetry, science.

The Junto members were pledged "to love truth for its own sake" and "to communicate the truth to others." They debated questions such as whether or not it is justifiable for the subject of a king to resist if his rights were taken away. Or, doesn't it demand hard study and work for a poor man to become rich if he would do it without becoming dishonest? Or, can any one particular form of government suit all mankind? And even, how can smoking chimneys best be cured?

Once every three months, members had to write an essay to be read to the group. Ben insisted on keeping discussions calm, avoiding hot arguments, "in the sincere spirit of inquiry of the truth." So successful was the Junto that many other men asked to join. But rather than enlarge beyond a dozen, Ben suggested that each member form a similar club if he liked, and five or six others under different names were established.

It was Ben's enthusiasm and genius that inspired and guided these clubs. They grew partly out of his sociable temperament. "I love company, chat, a laugh, a glass, and even a song," he said. No matter where he was, he always had friends and the time to see them. Besides the amusement and information they provided, the clubs formed ideas for improving life in town and colony, and they acted as a pressure group to bring about reforms. Their "wish to do good" not only improved society but benefited one another. Ben drew from the members material for his *Gazette* and trade for his business. The network served their pockets as well as their minds.

Since none could afford an extensive private library, they soon saw the value of pooling their books through the Junto. Out of it grew a circulating library for all the townfolk who would subscribe. Books they could not find in the colonies they imported from London, especially the works of John Locke, the philosopher whose economic and humanitarian interests and liberal views had done much to shape Ben's thinking.

Surely by now Ben knew how talented he was. Comparing himself with his fellows, he could see he was more imaginative, persistent, daring. Escaping from Boston at seventeen, he had proved he could tackle the world alone. Through his reading he had molded his own mind and then had begun to chart a course of personal discipline aimed at strengthening his moral character. "I wished to live without committing any faults at any time; I would conquer all that either natural inclination, custom or company might lead me into. As I knew, or thought I knew, what was right and wrong, I did not see why I might not always do the one and avoid the other. But I soon found I had undertaken a task of more difficulty than I had imagined. While my care was employed in guarding against one fault, I was often surprised by another; habit took advantage of inattention; inclination was sometimes too strong for reason."

He concluded that he had systematically to break bad habits and develop good ones. So he wrote down this list of thirteen virtues and what to do about each of them:

TEMPERANCE: Eat not to dullness, drink not to elevation.

SILENCE: Speak not but what may benefit others or yourself; avoid trifling conversation.

ORDER: Let all your things have their place; let each part of your business have its time.

RESOLUTION: Resolve to perform what you ought; perform without fail what you resolve.

FRUGALITY: Make no expense but to do good to others or yourself; i.e., waste nothing.

INDUSTRY: Lose no time; be always employed in something useful; cut off all unnecessary actions.

SINCERITY: Use no harmful deceit; think innocently and justly; and, if you speak, speak accordingly.

JUSTICE: Wrong none by doing injuries, or omitting the benefits that are your duty.

MODERATION: Avoid extremes; forbear resenting injuries so much as you think they deserve.

CLEANLINESS: Tolerate no uncleanliness in body, clothes, or habitation.

TRANQUILITY: Be not disturbed at trifles, or by accidents common or unavoidable.

CHASTITY: Rarely use venery but for health or offspring; never to dullness, weakness, or the injury of your own or another's peace or reputation.
HUMILITY: Imitate Jesus and Socrates.

Reading the list, we can't forget what a hot temper Ben had shown as a youngster, how willful and rash he had been, how careless his way with women. To us this list may sound as amusing as the annual New Year's resolutions. But Ben was in dead earnest. He kept a special notebook in which he recorded, week by week, the degree to which he lived up to each one of the virtues in turn. He was a man of his time, born into the optimistic Age of Enlightenment. Its thinkers believed virtue could be taught, that preaching it to the young would make a difference in their lives.

Long after, when in his late seventies, he said his virtues notebook had made him a better and a happier man. Still, he could laugh at himself over his weaknesses. Speaking of his vow of humility, he said:

In reality there is perhaps no one of our natural passions so hard to subdue as pride. Disguise it, struggle with it, beat it down, stifle it, mortify it as much as one pleases, it is still alive, and will every now and then peep out and show itself. . . . For even if I

could conceive that I had completely over-
come it, I should probably be proud of my
humility.

He came to see that perfection is not only impossible
but undesirable. It makes a man envied and hated.
A good man should permit himself a few faults, or
he will have no friends.

CHAPTER FIVE

POOR RICHARD'S ALMANACK

Everyone is familiar with almanacs—those books containing calendars, astronomical data, statistics, charts, tables, holidays, festivals, weather forecasting, and scraps of facts about anything the editor hopes the reader will like.

None is better known than *Poor Richard's Almanack*. It was concocted by Benjamin Franklin in 1732, three years after he launched his *Pennsylvania Gazette*. Already well-known and well-off, he increased his fame and fortune with *Poor Richard*. In those days, every shop, every farmhouse, every hunter's cabin had an almanac on the shelf, if no other book, for the facts and for the fun. In the almanacs they found astrological charts, weather predictions, oddities of history, recipes, jokes, poems, songs, advice. Printers published them as their staple product, for they would always put money in the till. Almanacs were written by "philomaths"—lovers of learning—and if they had a flair for catching the public fancy, success was certain.

When Ben decided to publish one, he did not hire a philomath. (Who knew more than he did?) Rather, he invented a character, "Richard Saunders, Philomath," and pretended it was this Richard who prepared the almanac.

Ben himself, only twenty-six, was not yet a household name, but his Richard soon was. As one Franklin biographer, Esmond Wright, puts it, Richard Saunders was "the voice of this new and growing society, the voice of the New Man in the New World." Ben did it by creating a new human character who figured in a series of almanacs he wrote annually for the next twenty-five years. To write a novel with Richard as the hero might have been another way of doing it. But novels were new on the scene in those days, and not a form Ben took to. It was easier and more natural for him to create this one personality, Richard Saunders. He introduced him to the public with such charm that Richard immediately became the favorite of the masses:

Courteous Reader:

I might in this place attempt to gain thy favor by declaring that I write almanacs with no other view than that of the public good, but in this I should not be sincere; and men are nowadays too wise to be deceived by pretenses, how specious soever. The plain truth of the matter is, I am excessive poor, and my wife, good woman, is, I tell her, excessive proud; she cannot bear, she says, to sit spinning in her shift of tow, while I do nothing but gaze at the stars; and has threatened more than once to burn all my books and rattling traps (as she calls my instruments) if I do not make some profitable use of them for the good of my family. The printer has offered me some considerable share of the profits, and I have thus begun to comply with my dame's desire.

Step by step he develops Poor Richard as an amusing character. In the next almanac Richard reports he's now somewhat better off. His wife has a pot of her own and no longer needs to borrow one from a neighbor. And best of all, they have something to put in it, which has made her less cranky. He plays with Richard's identity by disproving the accusation that Poor Richard isn't a real person. The astrology and weather forecasting so central to all almanacs he ridicules by an elaborate pretense of taking them seriously. From time to time he reports the ups and downs of his marriage, and once has his wife prepare the almanac herself.

Ben stole freely from other almanacs as well as from the writings of such literary men as Jonathan Swift, Laurence Sterne, and Rabelais. He packed

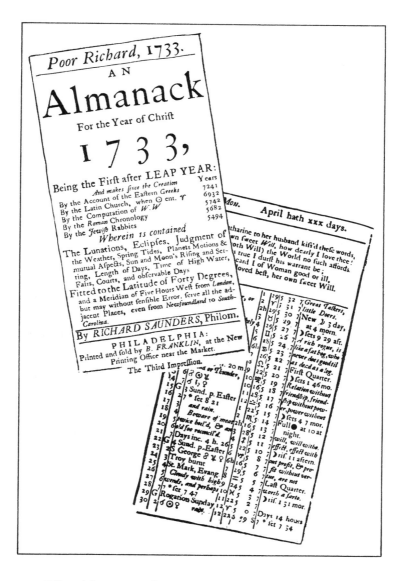

The title-page of Poor Richard's Almanack
for 1733, and a typical page inside

his pages with common sense and wise sayings, "gleanings," he said, "of all ages and nations. . . . Why should I give my readers bad lines of my own, when good ones of other people's are so plenty?" He was adept at taking another's lines and giving them a wry twist that enhanced their flavor and drove home their meaning. An English proverb goes, "God restoreth health and the physican hath the thanks." Ben turned it into, "God heals and the doctor takes the fee."

The down-home, humorous characters he invented made the *Almanack* a welcome addition to every home. "What Franklin provided," says Esmond Wright, "and what was his unique creation, was the fresh and authentic voice . . . of an all-too-believable, crotchety, quirkish and talkative character, the hen-pecked husband of a shrewish wife, Bridget. . . ."

Every autumn the *Almanack* readers dipped into Ben's rippling stream of fun:

Never spare the parson's wine, nor the baker's pudding.

Who had deceived thee so oft as thyself?

There is no little enemy.

It is hard for an empty sack to stand upright.

Necessity never made a good bargain.

Keep your eyes wide open before marriage, half shut afterwards.

Two lessons from one of the lavishly illustrated editions of Poor Richard

Poor Richard was an immediate hit. The first almanac ran through several printings, then the sales climbed to an annual figure of about ten thousand copies. That was one copy for every hundred Americans. (In today's America a comparable sale would be 2,400,000 copies.) Only the Bible exceeded *Poor Richard* in popularity. For Ben, *Poor Richard* built up a great reputation. It helped make possible the profound influence he would exert on the course of American political life.

In the twentieth century some critics would look at Poor Richard and see his creator, Ben Franklin, as a money-grubber, a rugged individualist who pinched pennies and thought only about getting ahead. They focus on the many maxims such as "God helps them that help themselves" and build a case against Franklin as the first Babbitt. Certainly the urge to do well for oneself has been a powerful theme in our society for a very long time. But when you look at Poor Richard, you are not looking at the whole Ben Franklin. You are looking at a fictional character, the conscious creation of a literary talent who is often satirizing the views of Poor Richard. Ben Franklin was real, far more complex than Poor Richard, and above all, a truly great man. As Carl Van Doren says, he was "a harmonious human multitude."

For twenty-five years Ben prepared the almanac himself. For his last edition, in the year 1758, he selected from all the previous editions about one hundred of Poor Richard's sayings and formed them into a preface. These sayings he puts into the mouth of an old man, Father Abraham, haranguing a crowd attending an auction. Ben punctures Poor Richard's moralizing balloon with one sharp sentence that comes at the end, when the effect upon the listening crowd is described: "The people heard it, and approved the doctrine, and immediately practiced the contrary, just as if it had been a common sermon." The preface was so universally liked that Ben printed it separately as *The Way to Wealth* and saw the pamphlet copied in newspapers throughout Europe. By now it has gone through some thirteen hundred editions. Translated into a great many languages, it made Poor Richard a quotable character for everyone from nobleman to newsboy.

To take the humdrum almanac form and raise it to the level of art is a considerable, if unexpected, achievement. Ben's literary inventiveness was strong enough to make Poor Richard a continuously interesting character who held a vast audience for a quarter of a century, and far beyond. So good is Franklin's prose that it is easier to quote him than to comment on him. "Clear, spare, simple, pungent, polished" are adjectives often used to describe his style.

These words characterize an American prose that anticipates Mark Twain. He has Twain's wit and humor, and like both Lincoln and Twain, could draw on a great collection of diverting stories. "Everything puts me in mind of a story," he wrote a friend. As but one example, when he had grown weary of working on a political issue to which he had given much time, he said:

> I begin to be a little of the sailor's mind when they were hauling a cable out of a store into a ship, and one of 'em said: "It's a long, heavy cable. I wish we could see the end of it." "Damn me," says another, "if I believe it has any end; somebody has cut it off."

Well, one more example. He hated the stupid practice of dueling, and protesting against it, cited the case of a gentleman in a coffeehouse who asked another gentleman to sit farther away from him:

> "Why so?"
> "Because, sir, you stink."
> "That is an affront, and you might fight me."
> "I will fight you, if you insist upon it, but I do not see how that will mend the matter. For if you kill me, I shall stink too; and if I kill you, you will stink, if possible, worse than you do at present."

Ben did a vast amount of writing from his boyhood to his death. The edition of his complete writing now in progress has reached volume 25, and at least twenty-five more volumes are expected.

Yet he himself never wrote a book, except for the *Autobiography*, which wasn't started with publication in mind. His works are mostly essays, letters, pamphlets, speeches, and scientific reports, written to meet some need of the moment, personal or public. Someone has suggested that he didn't have the patience to write a book. Yet he seemed never to be in a hurry. Look at his many portraits: almost all show him in repose—the look on his face, the relaxed body, the whole attitude.

So you cannot call him a literary man, not in the sense of one who makes a career of writing. Almost everything he wrote was done quickly and was rarely revised or even proofread. But the quality of what he wrote would have much to do with his success in many other fields.

IMPROVE YOURSELF,
IMPROVE YOUR COMMUNITY

Improve Yourself" was a motto Ben followed faithfully. Making the most of your abilities, however, could not be done in isolation. We are social creatures, he believed, and we live and grow within a community to which and for which we are responsible. We help ourselves by helping others.

Perhaps the earliest sign of that impulse occurred back in Ben's boyhood in Boston. Recall the time when he tried to improve fishing conditions for his gang by building a wharf into the pond. His interest in improvements was given depth and urgency when he read those essays on social projects by Cotton Mather and Daniel Defoe. In Philadelphia he started the Junto Club as a collective effort at self-improvement. It reached out into the community by starting the first circulating library in America, an idea that was soon copied throughout the colonies. It was followed by many other projects Ben designed for the public benefit.

These would begin when he saw something wrong in his surroundings. Take the condition of Philadelphia's streets. They were broad, straight, and regularly spaced—but unpaved. In wet weather the carriages and wagons plowed them into quagmires, and pedestrians had to wade in mud. In dry weather the dust choked everyone. It had been this way for a very long time, but no one thought to do anything about it—until Ben went into action. He took it one step at a time. First he talked about it. Then he wrote about it in his *Gazette*. When public opinion was ripe, he began with a small enterprise:

The Junto Club discusses a project.

he got a street in just one busy market block paved with stone. Ah, that was very nice; people noticed the happy difference and appreciated it. Then he found a man who was willing to sweep the pavement twice a week, carry off the dirt and garbage in front of all the houses and shops on that block, and do it for just sixpence per month, to be paid by each house.

Now Ben wrote and printed a leaflet setting out the advantages of such a cleaning system, to be done at small expense, stressing the benefits to the residents, to the shopkeepers and to their customers. He sent the leaflet to each house, and a day or so later went around to see who would consent to the proposal. Everyone signed up for it, and the cleaning job began. The whole town was delighted with the vastly improved condition of the market district, for it was a convenience for all. And, of course, he wrote, "This raised a general desire to have all the streets paved, and made the people more willing to submit to a tax for that purpose." This was the moment he was waiting for. He drew up a bill to pave the city. The Assembly passed it, even adding a provision for lighting as well as for paving the streets.

That is but one example of how Franklin saw the connection between what was good for himself and what was good for the community. He was able to tap the civic spirit of the people to draw them into a public organization of their town that would provide everyone with the decencies of civic life. Today we take these things for granted. But he was among the very first to come up with all kinds of plans and projects for getting something socially useful done.

Many of Franklin's projects were first tested in the Junto. He read a paper to his club on the careless ways houses were set on fire, with proposals for how to avoid such accidents. That led to the formation of a volunteer fire brigade. About thirty men soon joined, each equipped with leather water buckets and strong bags and baskets to carry out endangered furniture, and so on. They met monthly to exchange experience in firefighting and ideas on fire prevention, and, as Ben shrewdly saw, to enjoy a social evening together. The value of this first fire brigade led to one company after another being formed until the whole town was covered, with fire engines, ladders, and all the other necessary equipment stocked by each group. Ben was able to boast that no other city in the world was better prepared for fires than his Philadelphia.

What about a police force? All the town had was an amateurish watch system. Each ward had a constable who mustered a number of householders to serve with him for the night. You could get out of the civic duty by paying six shillings a year. The money was supposed to be used to hire substitutes, but much of it went into the constables' private purse and the rest bought drinks for "ragamuffins" who were too tipsy to walk their rounds.

*An old engraving shows Franklin's
volunteer fire company in action.*

Ben saw that the system failed to work. He wrote a paper for the Junto that proposed a more effective watch. Let's hire a full-time police force, he said, and support it by levying a tax on every citizen proportionate to the value of his property. Thus, the better off, who had most to lose by theft, would pay more than the poorer folk. He got the idea talked about, lined up other clubs to support it, and in a few years a law was adopted to carry it out.

A self-educated man, Franklin knew the value of providing a good education for every child. The Quakers ran some elementary schools in Philadelphia, but no college. There were still only three colleges throughout the colonies, none in Philadelphia and not even an academy. Ben discussed his ideas for higher education in the Junto and then wrote a pamphlet to spread his proposals. His views on education were liberal: he wanted to see science and other practical subjects taught, as well as the classical Greek and Latin. But knowing that this desire to change the old system would not be well received by the influential people he hoped to raise money from, he tempered his views to suit them. His pamphlet brought in a large sum of money, and within a year an academy was operating in a big building in the center of town. It met a real need and had plenty of students. Not forgetting his own childhood, Ben arranged for the academy to maintain a free school for poor children. Later the academy obtained a charter from the province and became a college. Today it is the University of Pennsylvania. It might better have been called Franklin University.

The academy was only one of Franklin's many projects to encourage education. He established elementary schools in half a dozen towns in the colony. For a time he chaired a committee devoted to founding schools for Blacks and Indians. He was in advance of his time in advocating better and more widespread education for women. When a printer he had set up as a partner in South Carolina died, and the man's widow took over the business, he was delighted to see her become so successful she was able to buy him out. She was an example he used on others. He thought greater stress on practical education for women so that they could make their own way in the world was better than lessons limited to music and dancing and the arts of catching a husband.

Not all such projects were his own idea. But he knew how to make a reality out of other people's hopes and dreams. A friend, Dr. Thomas Bond, conceived the idea of establishing a hospital in Philadelphia. That was such a novelty in America that Bond got nowhere with it. He came to Ben because he had seen that no public-spirited project was carried through without Franklin behind it. Ben liked the idea and went to work. He kept pushing the need for a hospital in the columns of his *Gazette*, then wrote a pamphlet outlining the proposal and the means to finance it. After some

The rebus was one of
Franklin's ingenious devices
for teaching a lesson.

astute political maneuvering, he got the Assembly to provide a grant. He used the device of the matching grant to get backing for the bill. If Philadelphians would subscribe a certain sum of money, the Assembly would match it.

Once the hospital was established, he kept a close eye on it, publicizing what it offered and presiding over its board. He always made sure to keep Philadelphians informed and involved. They were the hospital's patients, of course, but they were also its patrons and source of support.

What Ben learned as he pursued his public projects was a lesson he thought everyone could profit by. People don't like it, he said, when you put yourself forward as the proposer of any useful project they think might raise your reputation even a tiny degree above theirs. If you need their help, then it is best to keep yourself in the background. Make it appear that the project is the idea of a number of people who asked you to help launch it. That way it will go more smoothly. From his frequent successes with this method, he said he could "heartily recommend it." You may sacrifice your vanity for the moment, but afterward you are amply repaid. People will find out to whom the credit really belongs.

As printer and publisher, Ben was familiar with the most intimate daily dealings of the town. Himself in the center of things, it was inevitable that he quickly became one of Philadelphia's most prominent citizens. Early on, the General Assembly chose him to be its clerk. It was boring to sit through hours of dull speeches. But besides pay for the service, the clerkship put him in close touch with the members. And that brought him business—the printing of votes, laws, paper money, and other public work. All very profitable. The appointment also gave him influence with the Assembly; it helped advance his public projects. He held the position for nearly fifteen years.

In 1737 the postmaster general of the colonies made him deputy postmaster for Philadelphia. It was not a full-time job. He continued doing everything else. The post office was placed alongside his print shop and store. While it meant more work for Debby, she enjoyed getting the news first. In colonial times it was the person who received a letter who paid the postage. If he or she didn't have the money, the postmaster entered the debt on the books and tried to collect it when he could. It was Debby who kept those books.

The postmaster's salary was small, but the position was valuable to Ben. He could gather news for his *Gazette* more easily, and it cost him nothing to distribute the paper through his post-riders. With these advantages his subscriptions increased and so did his advertising.

Now he was very much a public figure: assembly clerk, postmaster, and sponsor of library, hospital, academy, college—all this while in his early thirties. How much money he made in his business enterprises it is hard to tell. It must have been considerable, for he was the most successful printer in British America, doing most of the printing for both the middle and the southern colonies.

During these same years, his mind was busy with scientific as well as civic projects. (More on these shortly.) How much can one man do? And what is the best use to make of your abilities? It is a hard choice that always confronts the talented. Some would say, let your personal preference take you where it will. In Franklin's century strong opinion held that the public welfare came first. To a scientist who wanted badly to retire, Ben wrote: "Had Newton been pilot of but a single ship, the finest of his discoveries would scarce have excused or atoned for his abandoning the helm one hour in time of danger; how much less if she carried the fate of the commonwealth!" Jefferson disagreed: "Nobody can conceive that nature ever intended to throw away a Newton upon the occupations of a crown."

It was the immediate threat of an invasion that thrust Ben into the center of political affairs. In the 1740s Britain got involved with France in a series of continental battles (King George's War, they called it.) Neither side pushed the war hard in America. But there were some engagements here, with the French and their Spanish or Indian allies making raids on English towns. In 1747 French and Spanish privateers sailed up the Delaware, sacked two plantations, and threatened Philadelphia. The Assembly was dominated by Quaker pacifists who refused to pass a bill to establish a militia. The other wealthy merchants were not eager to spend money to protect Quaker property. It made Ben think of the story about the man who "refused to pump in a sinking ship because one on board whom he hated would be saved by it as well as himself."

The town had been lucky up to now: the Quaker policy of friendship with the Indians had saved them from war for over fifty years. But it had left Philadelphia defenseless: no troops and no forts. Ben rushed to press with a pamphlet that argued it was the government's duty to protect the people and the people's duty to obey the government in this crisis. Unlike the Quakers, he didn't believe that man is inherently good and peaceful. But since the Quakers would not drop their religious pacifism and the merchants were selfishly blind to danger, the people must defend themselves. "The way to secure peace is to be prepared for war," he wrote. His call to arms won the governor's backing, and ten thousand men volunteered for a militia. They bought arms, drilled themselves, and elected their own officers. Ten regiments were formed in the town and another hundred in the colony. To finance the defense Ben organized a lottery that paid for the erection of a battery and the purchase of guns from Boston.

The militia asked Ben to be their regimental colonel, but he thought he was not fit, and refused. His boldness and his initiative in rising to the challenge of defense made him immensely popular throughout the colony. Again he showed that good citizenship took cooperative action. If the Assembly would not move, then the people must. The peace treaty of 1748 in Europe soon ended the threat of invasion, and the militia faded away. What Ben did to mobilize the Pennsylvanians foreshadowed how public-minded citizens would act together in a democratic way when their liberties were in danger.

He did all these things with such tact and skill that he made few enemies. But the public man was not yet a public official. That would be the next step.

In 1748 Ben decided to retire from business. At the age of forty-two (it proved to be halfway through his long life), he had made enough to be able to do it. This after working for himself for only twenty years. He brought into partnership his foreman, David Hall. Hall would run the printing and publishing business, now renamed Franklin and Hall, at a salary of £1000 a year. The agreement assured Ben of a comfortable living for the life of the partnership, set at eighteen years, when Hall would become sole owner. During that time, Ben received from the profits an average of £500 per year.

Did that mean he was rich? Yes, if you compare his income with others. In his day, a housemaid was paid £10 a year, a clerk £25, a teacher £60. The chief justice of the colony got £200 per year, and the highest official, the governor, £1,000. Remember that Ben was a partner in print shops in other colonies, too, and had income from the post office and real estate, as well as from financial investments.

He was not a greedy man; business of itself gave him no joy. It was only a means to carry out his other goals. Wealth to him meant freedom to do what he wanted, freedom to be useful to the community. He would not retire from public life, only from private enterprise.

And best of all, he would be able to give much more time to his passion for scientific research.

CHAPTER SEVEN

INVENTOR AND SCIENTIST

To be forty-two in Ben Franklin's time was to be well beyond middle age. Life was much shorter then. He never guessed he would live double those years. Since retirement was not forced upon him, he felt no depression for cutting himself off from his work. He moved his family from Market Street to a more spacious rented house. It was on the northwest corner of Race and Second, a quieter part of town, and nearer to the river. Although he did not live luxuriously, he acquired slaves to help with the household chores and errands.

Now he was ready to plunge headlong into his life as a scientist. Science as a way of exploring and explaining the world was a path he had entered long ago. Recall how his inventiveness was revealed in boyhood when he devised new ways to speed himself through water. At twenty, sailing back from England, he had crammed his notebook with observations of wind and weather and ocean currents and animal life. His scientific curiosity could be

aroused by what others brushed off as trivial. Once
he found that an open pot of molasses in Debby's
pantry was crawling with ants. He removed all of
them but one, then tied the pot to a string suspended from the ceiling, led the string across the
ceiling and down the wall, and sat by to observe.
The one ant gorged itself in the pot, then clambered
along the string and down the wall, and disappeared. About thirty minutes later, the pot was
once again thick with ants that had crossed over to
it on the string. How, Ben asked, had the first ant
communicated to the others the feast awaiting them
in the pot?

Again and again he saw in everyday aspects of
nature questions that demanded answers. Where
others before him had noticed nothing interesting
or significant, his mind saw something wonderful.
He was born to be a "natural philosopher," the
term used then for scientists.

It was Sir Francis Bacon who began the turn
toward modern science. In 1620—the same year
the Puritan dissenters fled England to find refuge
in New England—he published the first statement
of a new attitude. It would change the way people
lived in the world and the way they thought about
it. Bacon believed the whole world was open for
genius to explore. The object of knowledge was to
increase man's power over nature and to make life
better. Only by a true understanding of the physical
world could we master our fate.

Later, in 1662, Bacon's followers founded the

Royal Society in London "to promote the welfare of the arts and sciences." The great Isaac Newton, one of the Society's original members, had shown that the universe moved by its own laws and that mathematics could chart those movements of the planets. Only a few Americans, Cotton Mather among them, were familiar with science. Mather, when Franklin was fifteen, had published America's first popular book on science. He wanted people to break from stale myths and go out and dig for the truth in the real world of nature. It was an appeal young Ben responded to.

Scientific research back then was vastly different from what it is now. In Ben's time it was an amateur's game. No government, no corporation, no university, no foundation was on hand to pour funds into research. Scientists—the few there were—did not combine their specialized knowledge to work together in large laboratories under ideal conditions. Nor was there any kind of training for them in research. Like Ben, they taught themselves and worked alone, usually at home, funding their own expenses. It was a kind of game, but with an intellectual edge that gave it great excitement, especially when you could claim a discovery.

Several months after he retired, Ben wrote to his friend Cadwallader Colden that he was happy "to make experiments, and converse at large with such ingenious and worthy men as are pleased to honor me with their friendship on such points as may produce something for the common benefit of mankind, uninterrupted by the little cares and fatigues of business."

Years earlier Ben had suggested that people interested in science ought to form an organization "to promote useful knowledge" in the colonies. His notion was to expand the Junto on a continental scale. He had already corresponded with scientists throughout the colonies, as well as with some in England and Europe. He knew how rapidly interest in science was growing and saw that pooling information and ideas would greatly benefit everyone. He wrote out his proposal in 1743 and printed and circulated it. Out of it came the American Philosophical Society. It is the oldest American learned society, and the first to be devoted to science. Ben's desire was to make it a center for exchanging information on all aspects of the natural world and on all experiments that "tend to increase the power of man over matter, and multiply the conveniences or pleasures of life." Franklin became its first president, to be followed later by Thomas Jefferson and other distinguished Americans. Today, as at its founding, it concerns itself with many diverse fields of knowledge—medicine, physics, anthropology, history, literature—and its publications and projects are important to the international world of science.

A look through the pages of Ben's *Gazette* shows how early it began to reflect the range of his scientific curiosity. Esmond Wright has traced his stories of "the weather and waterspouts; why salt dissolves in water; why the sea is sometimes luminous; cures for kidney stones and cancer; mortality rates in Philadelphia; the cause of earthquakes; 'on making rivers navigable'; how many people could stand in an area of 100 square yards."

Ben's voracious appetite for learning made him ask the why and how of everything he came across. When he was still tied down by his business, he did his best to encourage others in the pursuit of science. For instance, he raised a fund to enable John Bartram, a botanist, to continue his research on the condition that he report his findings to contributors to the fund.

In Franklin's mind there was nothing that could not be improved. Take his invention of the Franklin stove. One of the questions he had posed for the Junto was, "How may smoky chimneys be cured?" How strange it was, he thought, that while chimneys have been so long in use, no workman would pretend he could make one that would carry off all the smoke. Then, too, fireplaces were often too hot to sit near, and when you did, while the heat toasted your front, the cold air nipped your back and legs. It was next to impossible to warm a room with such a fireplace. So in 1739 or 1740 he invented a stove that fitted into the fireplace and radiated the heat outward. It warmed rooms better, and at the same time saved fuel. The important feature was the flue, which doubled back and formed a sort of radiator around which warm air circulated. It cured

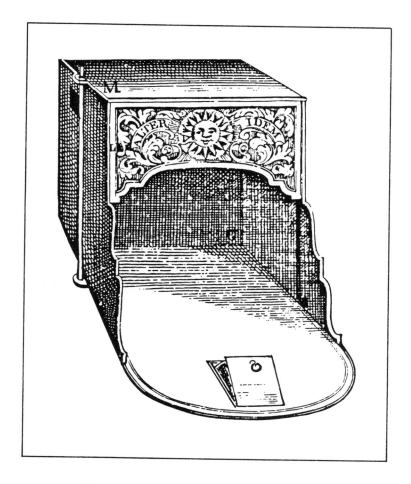

*One component of Franklin's famous
stove, designed before he began his
electrical experiments. The key element
was the flue: it doubled back to spread
the heat into the room, rather than
sending it up the chimney and out.*

most smoky chimneys, thus protecting both the eyes and the furniture. He turned over his model to a friend with an iron furnace, who cast the plates for the stoves. They were soon in great demand as people learned about them through a pamphlet Ben wrote and printed.

A profitable invention—but not for him. As with all his inventions, he refused to patent his stove, on the principle "that as we enjoy great advantages from the inventions of others, we should be glad of an opportunity to serve others by any invention of ours, and this we should do freely and generously."

He was as much interested in ventilating rooms as in warming them. He believed it healthier to keep windows open and let in fresh air, a practice that annoyed many of his friends. To keep rooms warmer in cold weather, he developed a damper, a metal plate that fits horizontally into the base of the chimney passage and can completely close it off, or when opened a small distance, creates a slight draft, allowing smoke to go up the chimney while keeping most of the warm air in the room.

To improve the lighting of rooms, he devised a new candle made from whale oil. It gave a clearer and whiter light, could be held in the hand without softening, and its drippings did not make grease spots. His candles lasted much longer and needed little or no snuffing. He also developed a four-sided lamp to light the city streets. The lamps stayed clean much longer and thus gave more light.

When Franklin's scientific fame comes up, most people think of the spectacular kite experiment. That was not his greatest contribution, and it was made well after his international reputation was established. Most important was his experimental approach: it was this that made all his contributions possible. His experiments in so many different fields were completely original and crucial. The way he went about his research displayed his analytic powers and his objectivity. He never rested with merely amplifying what someone else had done.

His work on electricity is the best example. Before he began to think about it, electricity was a mass of uncoordinated observations and confusing theories worded in obscure and puzzling language. Franklin's mind was able to unify what was already known, then to add his own original findings so that he came out with a new and simple theory that would stand the test of time. The very vocabulary of modern electricity originated with him: as he went along he had to invent words like *condenser, conductor, charge, discharge, armature, battery, electrician, electric shock, positive* and *negative* electricity, and concepts of *plus* and *minus* charges.

Few of his contemporaries were equipped to perceive how different and advanced his approach was. Those who did understand his work thought it extraordinary. By the time Ben went abroad on his first diplomatic mission (1757), scientists in England and Europe greeted him as the Newton of electricity.

The Ben Franklin who earned that reputation was not the Franklin we know from the famous portraits of him in later years. These show him as portly or dumpy, stringy haired or bald. The Franklin of his pioneering years in science was a tall, muscular man with chestnut hair and an enigmatic smile. Charming and witty, Ben at that time was equalled by no one in the variety of his accomplishments. A physicist sees Franklin's uniqueness in "an intellect that could penetrate through a morass of detail to the one underlying simplicity. Of all human talents, it is the most uncommon, even though men flatter themselves by calling it common sense."

The first spark to ignite Ben's interest in "the mysterious fluid" called electricity was struck on a visit to Boston in 1743. There he met Dr. Archibald Spencer from Scotland who was traveling around the colonies to display his repertoire of tricks in electrostatics. His most spectacular stunt was to suspend a small boy from the ceiling by silken threads while he drew sparks from the child's hands and feet. The audiences for these shows were both fascinated and frightened. Ben said that what he witnessed had "surprised and pleased" him as a quite new subject. He invited Spencer to display his "shocks" and "magic" in Philadelphia and bought his apparatus. Then, with the help of the Junto and the library company, he tried some experiments. Ben asked the botanist Peter Collinson, a member of the Royal Society, to send him a glass "electric tube," with directions for using it in making experiments. He eagerly set out to repeat what he had learned and then developed new experiments. His house was "continually full for some time with people who came to see these new wonders. . . . I was never before engaged in any study that so totally engrossed my attention and my time," he wrote Collinson as he provided details on what he was trying to do. Already he was transforming the electrical parlor games into a science.

Part of the standard equipment of electrical experiments at that time was the Leyden jar. It was simply a stoppered bottle of water. Through the cork stopper a metal rod hung down into the liquid. Some experimenters coated the bottle on the outside with metal foil. When charged, the Leyden jar gave a strong shock to people touching it. In one experiment to enlighten the French court, when a shock was given to a line of 180 guardsmen, all holding hands, they jumped simultaneously into the air as though parading in the sky. The same experiment at a monastery threw seven hundred monks into a whirling convulsion.

Here is how a twentieth-century physicist, Mitchell Wilson, explains the significance of Franklin's Leyden jar experiments:

Franklin set himself the task of answering a question which no one else had thought of asking: exactly what was it in such an ap-

parently simple arrangement of glass, metal,
and water that allowed for such enormous
accumulations of electricity? Was it due to
the wire, the water or the bottle? Or what
combination? In Franklin's day, no one even
knew, once the questions had been asked,
how to go about finding the answer. Actually,
to ask the same question two centuries after
Franklin would leave an embarrassingly
large number of people looking blank.
Franklin's step-by-step approach had the
simplicity of genius:

"To analyze the electrified bottle, in order
to find wherein its strength lay, we placed it
on glass and drew out the cork and wire.
. . . Then taking the bottle in one hand, and
bringing a finger of the other near the
bottle's mouth, a strong spark came from
the water . . . which showed that the force
did not reside in the wire."

And so one possibility was completely
eliminated.

"Then to find if it resided in the water
. . . which had been our former opinion, we
electrified the bottle again." This time,
Franklin and his assistant removed the cork
and the wire as before, and then in addition
decanted the water from the electrically
charged flask into another flask which had
not been electrified. If the electric charge

actually was in the water alone, then the new flask should give a spark. It did not.

"We judged then, that it must be lost in decanting or remain in the first bottle. The latter we found to be true, for that bottle on trial gave the shock, though filled with fresh, electrified water from a teapot."

Now, having come this far, not one man in a hundred thousand would have gone on to the next question, which was this: did the electrical charge reside in the bottle because it was shaped like a bottle or because it was made of glass? Again, one may well ask how could that be tested? Franklin took glass of a completely different shape: a simple pane of window glass. On either side of the glass, he placed a thin sheet of lead. This arrangement was electrified. Then, one at a time, the sheets of lead were slid away and tested. Neither, when isolated, gave off any spark. The glass pane, standing alone, being touched, gave off a multitude of sparks. Franklin then concluded that "The whole force and power of giving a shock is in the glass itself. . . ."

This proof that the seat of electrostatic action is in the material which insulates a conductor laid the foundation for Maxwell's work a century later when he developed the theory of electromagnetic waves which in turn led to radio. In this one experiment alone, Franklin had invented the electrical condenser, one of the most useful elements in circuit theory, a device that was to be used in every radio, television set, telephone circuit, radar transmitter, cyclotron and cosmotron.

Until Franklin, the prevalent theory had been that there were two different kinds of electricity vaguely distinguished by unanalytical names as resinous and vitreous. He claimed that there was only one kind; that electricity was neither created nor destroyed either by friction or by any other means, but that electricity was simply redistributed throughout matter. Moreover, he stated that electricity had to be composed of "subtile particles" that could penetrate the interior of metals as easily as gas diffused through the atmosphere. J. J. Thomson, who later discovered the electron and laid the foundations of modern electron theory, paid tribute to Franklin as generously as Franklin's own contemporaries.

Ben wrote several letters to Collinson describing his experiments, and the botanist got them read to the Royal Society. Ben's reports took an amusing turn at times:

The hot weather coming on when electrical experiments are not so agreeable, it is proposed to put an end to them for this season [spring 1749], somewhat humorously, in a party of pleasure on the banks of the Schuylkill. Spirits, at the same time, are to be fired by a spark sent from side to side through the river, without any other conductor than the water; an experiment which we some time since performed, to the amazement of many. A turkey is to be killed for our dinner by the electrical shock, and roasted by the electrical jack, before a fire kindled by the electrified bottle; when the healths of all the famous electricians in England, Holland, France and Germany are to be drunk in electrified bumpers, under the discharge of guns from the electrical battery.

Thus, he put his discoveries to use, though in this case only to entertain. Always he believed in a worldwide collaboration of scientists, advancing their common interest by the free exchange of information. He wanted even "short hints and imperfect experiments" to be reported, for anything might lead others to more complete and accurate discoveries. In 1751 Ben's accounts of his experiments were published in London in an eighty-six-page pamphlet called *Experiments and Observations on Electricity Made at Philadelphia in America by Mr. Benjamin Franklin.* He wrote in simple, direct, and clear language so that all could understand. The work was translated into several languages and built his European reputation as a scientist.

EXPERIMENTS
AND
OBSERVATIONS
ON
ELECTRICITY,
MADE AT
Philadelphia in *America,*
BY
Mr. BENJAMIN FRANKLIN,
AND
Communicated in several Letters to Mr. P. COLLINSON,
of *London,* F. R. S.

L O N D O N:
Printed and sold by E. CAVE, at *St. John's Gate.* 1751.
(Price 2s. 6d.)

*Title-page of the
first publication of
Franklin's experiments
in electricity*

What gave Franklin's pamphlet even greater celebrity was the success of one of the experiments he proposed to determine whether or not the clouds that contain lightning are electrified. He suggested that on top of some high tower, a sentry box be placed, big enough to contain a man standing on an insulated platform. "From the middle of the stand let an iron rod rise and pass bending out of the door, and upright 20 or 30 feet pointed very sharp at the end. If the electrical stand be kept clean and dry, a man standing on it when such clouds are passing low might be electrified and draw sparks, the rod drawing fire . . . from a cloud."

This he proposed in July 1750. He planned to perform the lightning experiment after the completion of the spire on Christ Church in Philadelphia. But meantime, his pamphlet was published in France and made a strong impression. Thomas Francis D'Alibard, a scientist, made a secret trial of the sentry box experiment near Paris on May 10, 1752. There was a peal of thunder, and the iron shaft sparkled blue with charge pouring into a Leyden jar, proving that the cloud was electrified. Shortly afterward, the experiment was repeated for the king in Paris, and then again in London. By the time news of the proofs reached Franklin, he had been world famous for months.

For almost fifty years before Franklin, people had been suggesting that lightning and the electric spark were one and the same thing. But no one had ever worked out a way of proving it. Ben not only proposed an actual experiment, but he was also able to explain lightning rationally. No longer could it be viewed as an awesome expression of the supernatural.

Meanwhile, before he knew of the successful experiments in Europe, he decided not to wait for the church spire to be completed. It occurred to him that a common kite would be better able to reach the regions of a thunderstorm. With the help of his son William, then about twenty-two, he built a kite out of a large silk handkerchief and two cross-sticks. To the upright stick of the cross he tied a sharp pointed wire, rising about a foot above the wood. To the end of the string he fastened a silk ribbon and a key. When signs of a storm approached, they walked out into the fields. William

An artist imagines the famous kite
experiment and gets it all wrong.
Franklin didn't wear a fur hat until he
was an old man, his son was not a child
then, but a man of twenty, and the
Leyden jar is held in the wrong hand.

ran three times across a pasture to get the kite aloft while Ben watched from a shepherd's hut nearby. With the kite flying, there was an anxious time before any sign came of its being electrified. One promising cloud passed over it without any effect. Then, just as Ben despaired of any result, he saw some loose threads of the hempen string stand erect, avoiding one another as though they had been suspended on a common conductor. Struck with this promising appearance, Ben touched his knuckle to the key at his end of the kite string and—an exquisite moment of pleasure!—perceived an electric spark. His discovery was complete, even before the string was wet. When the rain had soaked the string, he collected a great amount of electric fire.

This happened in June 1752, a month after the French proof of his idea, but before he heard of anything they had done.

CHAPTER EIGHT

DISARMING THE CLOUDS OF HEAVEN

Now that the theory of the sameness of electricity and lightning had been confirmed, Ben did what came naturally: he put the knowledge to immediate use. He proposed the lightning rod as the way to protect structures from the stroke of lightning. By fixing sharply pointed iron rods to the highest part of a structure and extending from them a wire down the outside of the building into the ground, the electricity would be drawn silently out of the cloud before it came near enough to strike, and "thereby secure us from that most sudden and terrible mischief."

He put up a lightning rod on the roof of his own house, and soon they were put up on Philadelphia's new academy and the new State House. Again, he would not patent his invention to draw profit from it. Instead he described how to secure protection through lightning rods in the *Poor Richard* of 1753 so that anyone could do it freely. He was happy to make his idea useful to others. Not

Excitement in Philadelphia as an electrical storm
crackles over the first lightning rod,
mounted on the house of Benjamin West

everyone approved of "Franklin's rod," as it was
called. Even twenty years later someone wrote that
"as lightning is one of the means of punishing the
sins of mankind and of warning them from the
commission of sin, it *is* impious to prevent its full
execution."

For a time many hesitated to erect lightning
rods for fear they would bring down upon themselves the wrath of the Lord. But the practical
success of the invention eventually overcame all
resistance. Nothing enlarged Ben's reputation so
much as the lightning rod. Because it is more than
two hundred years in the past, it is hard for us to
realize the impact it had on people of that time.
Ben's contemporary, John Adams, can tell us how
his world viewed it:

> Nothing, perhaps, that ever occurred upon
> the earth was so well calculated to give any
> man an extensive and universal a celebrity
> as . . . the invention of lightning-rods. The
> idea was one of the most sublime that ever
> entered a human imagination, that a mortal
> should disarm the clouds of heaven. . . . His
> [lightning rods] erected their heads in all
> parts of the world, on temples and palaces
> no less than on cottages of peasants and
> habitations of ordinary citizens. These visible
> objects reminded all men of the name and
> character of their inventor; and in the course
> of time have not only tranquillized the minds

and dissipated the fears of the tender sex
and their timorous children, but have almost
annihilated that panic, terror and supersti-
tious horror which was once almost universal
in violent storms of thunder and lightning.

When others disagreed with Franklin or criticized
his research, he would make no reply. He refused
to defend his scientific views: "I leave them to take
their chance in the world. If they are right, truth
and experience will support them; if wrong, they
ought to be refuted and rejected."

Out of his loving investigation of nature came
not a single book about science. There were few
scientific journals then, and Ben's findings were
usually presented through letters to friends with
like interests. The public affairs in which he soon
became immersed and his long years as diplomat
in England and France left him little time for his
passion to investigate. But he never stopped ob-
serving nature, gathering facts, finding connections, interpreting them, and recording what he
learned. Always, it should be noted, in homely
language that reads as freshly today as when it was
penned. If only a Franklin were here to write the
modern textbooks in science!

In 1753 both Harvard and Yale gave Ben
honorary degrees, and a year later the Royal Society
awarded him the Copley Gold Medal. In the years
ahead he would be made a member of thirty-eight
learned societies and academies. Today's scientists

are no less impressed by Ben's achievements. And he did what he did with no technical training. When the Nobel Laureate Robert Millikan offered his personal rating of the great scientists from the sixteenth century to the twentieth, he placed Franklin fifth, after Copernicus, Galileo, Newton, and Huygens.

While carrying on his own studies, Ben was in frequent correspondence with many other scientists, both in America and Europe. He shared his interests with them and established lifelong friendships with many distinguished men in England and France. Although he valued his scientific honors, he seldom referred to them and even poked fun at them, once calling "a feather in the cap not so useful a thing as a pair of good silk garters." When he was invited to become a corresponding member of the Royal Society, he replied that he esteemed the honor and was not discouraged by the fact that "as yet, the quantity of human knowledge bears no proportion to the quality of human ignorance."

Franklin's contributions were so extensive as to make him the supreme scientist in the American colonies. He was viewed as a Renaissance man. Noting his genius, Charles L. Mee, Jr., lists a few of his characteristic interests:

Franklin had always been the sort of man who could, in the space of a single brief letter, cover such topics as linseed oil, hemp land, swamp drainage, variations in climate, northeast storms, the cause of springs on mountains, seashell rocks, grass seed, taxation, and smuggling. He loved facts. He loved the particular. He was able to talk with knowledge and cheerful interest about mastodon tusks, lead poisoning, chimney construction, the reason canal boats move more slowly in low water than in high water, silk culture, Chinese rhubarb seeds, sunspots, magnetism, a new method for making carriage wheels, the electrocution of animals to be eaten, how to heat a church in Boston, the census in China, the vegetable origins of coal, and the good of keeping a window in the bedroom open at night.

Philadelphia was fertile soil for the cultivation of Ben's scientific interests. He was surrounded by ingenious mechanics and artisans eager to perfect their craft and improve their product. Their love of tinkering was typical of that era. Several of those men, as we saw, were active in the Junto. Some, like David Rittenhouse, earned reputations as scientists that carried their names across the Atlantic. Rittenhouse, a clock-maker by trade, developed great skill in making mathematical instruments and became a famous astronomer. Ben's own talent for experiment was constantly stimulated by the company of such men. Thomas Jefferson wrote that Franklin, Rittenhouse, and George Washington were proof that America could nurture genius.

To describe in detail Franklin's discoveries needs a book unto itself. But just to list some of them will indicate the range of his observations and experiments. To start with the simpler things—those he made himself. He is credited with clocks, the stove, the lightning rod, astronomical instruments, bifocal eyeglasses, the flexible catheter, a chair that can be converted into a ladder, a clothes-pressing machine, improvements in the printing press, a pole with a manipulable grasp at the end to take down books from high shelves, laboratory equipment, the musical instrument called the "glass harmonica" for which Mozart and Beethoven wrote music. (He could, by the way, play the harp, the guitar, and the violin.)

The qualities of his mind are illustrated by his attention to many aspects of nature. Even the most casual incident was enough to set his mind spinning. In his eight crossings of the Atlantic he recorded things he saw at sea. One of the most important was the existence of the Gulf Stream, which he was the first scientist to study. It began in 1745 when he puzzled over why ships had much shorter voyages from America to England than in returning. Inquiring of sea captains, he learned that they were aware of the Gulf Stream and how it affected voyages. But Ben knew that no notice had been taken of this current upon the navigational charts. So he had a captain mark out the stream for him, adding directions for how to avoid it when sailing from Europe to North America. Then Ben had it engraved upon new charts and sent copies to sea captains who, he said wryly, "ignored it, however."

It was Ben who first suggested that the aurora borealis was an electrical phenomenon. He theorized on the origin of many things from colds to earthquakes. He demonstrated the way dark- or light-colored clothing increased or diminished how hot the wearer felt. His observations on the direction of storms began the modern study of weather. And he was the first to test the use of oil to quiet troubled waters.

One of his more significant innovations was the investigation of population changes that led to the new science of demography. It began with his observations in 1750 of the increase of pigeons. A year later he wrote the essay, "Observations Concerning the Increase of Mankind, Peopling of Countries, etc." Published in America and in London, it showed that population was increasing faster in the colonies than in Britain. Although his data were scanty, he forecast with great accuracy that the American population would shoot up enormously by a doubling of numbers every generation. It meant that in a hundred years there would be more people in America than in the mother country.

What this pointed to, he said, was that the colonies would be a "glorious market" for manufactured goods well beyond the capacity of England to fulfill. And therefore colonial manufacture should not be restricted, as it was under the mer-

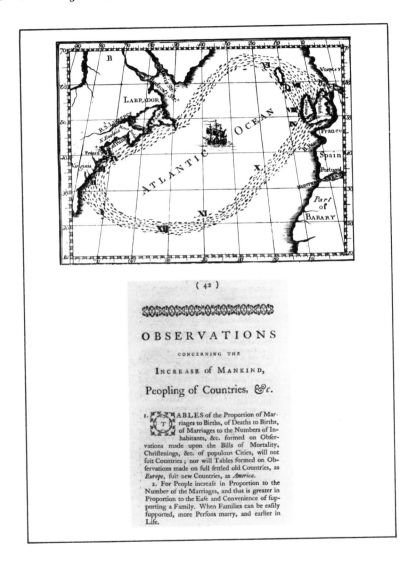

*Franklin's chart of the Gulf Stream and
a page from his essay on population*

cantilist system. He was not seeking a rupture with the home country; he still saw the colonies as part of the British Empire—but a part with a vast potential that "a wise and good mother" would not harm. He foresaw that American manufacturing would have to increase to satisfy the needs of the rapidly growing population. And he predicted that the frontier territory would provide an escape for the poor of the colonies, giving them a place to settle their large families on free and uncrowded land. Ben based his calculations on tables of births and deaths. (There would be no official census in America until 1790, the year of his death.)

One sorry aspect of his views on population is the racism that was common to his time, even among the most enlightened, such as Thomas Jefferson. Franklin was extremely ethnocentric. He did not welcome nonwhites to America, or even whites who were not English. The German settlers in western Pennsylvania upset him. He didn't like the way they clung to their own language and customs, and feared they would become so numerous as to "Germanize us, instead of our Anglifying them." He worried over the fact that white people were a relatively small part of the population of the earth. Why plant in America the dark, the tawny, the swarthy people? he asked. He discouraged their immigration. Then, perhaps feeling a twinge of guilt or shame over this point of view, he added, "But perhaps I am partial to the complexion of my country, for such kind of partiality is natural to mankind."

Among Franklin's many pursuits in science was a lifelong interest in medicine. Its condition in colonial America was far from medicine today. Formal training was almost unknown, and licensing did not exist. In fact, medicine was not yet a profession. Some learned the art by serving as apprentices to established doctors. But many simply declared themselves doctors and set themselves up in practice. Surgeons were thought to be the lowest doctors of all because they worked with their hands.

Experimental medicine, whether in laboratory or clinic, was a rarity. Franklin, always the realist, wanted to test every belief and practice. He looked for practical results, not old wives' tales about medical miracles. If an experiment proved an idea of his was wrong, he was quick to admit it. During his experiments with electricity, he tried applying it to stiff or paralyzed joints, but when no improvement was noted, he stopped the treatment. In his time few people were concerned with personal cleanliness. Ben advised stripping off your clothes and scrubbing yourself clean in a tub of water. Shocking! said his contemporaries. He designed and built his own copper bathtub, with a rack to hold a book so he could read while bathing. He advised moderation in eating and drinking, and regular exercise to keep fit. His ardent demand for fresh air and ventilation made him a nuisance to people who had to share a room with him.

His low view of the medical profession was expressed in some of his sayings: "God heals and the doctor takes the fee." Or, "He is the best physician that knows the worthlessness of most medicines." Yet some of his closest friends in America and in Europe were medical men. Perhaps because they were often radicals? So many doctors were active in the American Revolution that they made up almost an army of doctor-patriots. One estimate holds that nearly twelve thousand were involved in the cause. The reason is uncertain. It may be that they supported revolutionary politics because they were committed to science and reason.

Franklin did not hesitate to expose charlatans in science or quacks in medicine. On the other hand, he gave all the help he could to worthy scientists. In 1745 he aided Peter Kalm, the Swedish naturalist who had come to the colonies to search for botanical specimens unique to America. And in 1779, while Ben was serving as American commissioner to France, he protected the exploring expedition of British Captain James Cook, who was liable to capture at sea because of the war between Britain and America. Franklin notified all American naval vessels not to consider Cook an enemy or to obstruct his scientific mission in any way.

The list of Franklin's innovations could go on and on. He suggested daylight saving time. He was the first to introduce cartoons and the use of the question-and-answer format into journalism. He advocated adding to the traditional Latin and Greek the teaching of modern foreign languages. To promote the international spread of knowledge, he invented a language of symbols all peoples could use. He figured out a way to put Indian languages into print although the tribes had no written symbols. To get rid of the bewildering confusion of English spelling, he prepared "A Scheme for a New Alphabet and Reformed Mode of Spelling." Calling war a mass form of theft and murder, he advocated the idea of punishing aggressor nations through the organization of a United Nations.

CHAPTER NINE

A PLAN FOR UNION

The driving motive for Franklin's retirement from business in 1748 was the pursuit of science. But politics began to dominate his life even before he quit the printing trade. While science would remain his first love, it often had to give way to politics. The two were really linked in his mind, for each was an expression of his humanitarianism. A dozen years before the 1748 decision, he took his first political step when he was chosen clerk of the Pennsylvania legislature. Now he began his rise in elected office when he was voted into the city's Common Council in 1748, and in 1751, the Pennsylvania Assembly.

He did not seek office. The public, he said, "considering me as a man of leisure, laid hold of me for their purposes." He liked sitting in the legislature because he saw that it "would enlarge my power of doing good." But he confessed he was also "flattered by all these promotions. For considering my low beginning, they were great things to me." And it was still more pleasing for being entirely unsolicited.

Year after year he was reelected to the Assembly, always without campaigning. He served on many of its committees, attending to all kinds of public business. Underlying most issues was the running conflict between the Assembly and the governor, who was appointed and controlled by the Penn family.

The Penns were called the "proprietors" because they really owned the colony. It was not the king but William Penn and his descendants who ruled Pennsylvania. The vast lands of the colony had been given to William Penn by Charles II in payment of a debt he owed Penn's father. All the landholders were therefore under Penn domain and had to pay annual quitrents to the Penn family. So Pennsylvania from its very beginning was a kind of feudal state. There was an elected legislature, the Assembly, but it had only as much voice in government as the Penns granted it. Limited in authority, the Assembly battled with the governor, who represented not the people but the proprietors.

After Penn's death, his sons, who remained in England and were no longer Quakers, acted like feudal lords, concerned only to milk the province of all the revenue they could. They drew income from leases and quitrents while insisting that their own lands could not be taxed by the legislature.

The Pennsylvanians did not like it. It was their labor that was making the proprietors fat and prosperous, increasing regularly the value of their land. Why shouldn't the Penns help pay the cost of the government? No, said the Penns; the law is on our side. But reason and justice are on ours, the Pennsylvanians replied.

The conflict sharpened when the Indians in the western region grew troubled by the threat of settlers on their land. That region (now western Pennsylvania and eastern Ohio) was claimed by both Pennsylvania and Virginia. Traders had already entered, with white settlers sure to follow. Adding to the tension were the movements of both England and France, competing for territory to extend their own empires. The Indians, a kind of buffer between them, feared invasion from both sides. The English were drifting west across the mountains, and the French were heading down the Ohio Valley. The two European powers, at peace for the moment, tried to swing the Indians to their sides with lavish gifts.

The high cost of dealing with the Indians placed a burden on the Pennsylvanians. Going over the head of the governor, the Assembly wrote to the Penns, asking them to share the Indian expenses; the Penns refused. In this, as in other major negotiations, Franklin played a major role. Not in debate: he rarely spoke on the floor because he thought he didn't do it very well. Rather, he worked backstage, exploring opinions, reconciling differences, and then making a compelling case in writing for the compromise he usually could work out.

In their struggle to limit the governor's powers, the legislators spoke more and more vigorously for the rights and liberties of the people. Hold to what we think are the rights of the people we represent, said Franklin. It's that spirit of liberty that has gloriously distinguished the English from the rest of the world.

Within a couple of years Franklin was recognized as the power in the Assembly—to the disgust of the Penns. His authority was magnified when the Royal Society awarded him a medal, and Yale and Harvard gave him honorary degrees. And in that same year—1753—he was named deputy postmaster general of all the colonies.

His appointment as postmaster general did not come out of the blue. Knowing that the man holding the job was quite sick, Franklin got Peter Collinson, his botanist friend in London, and William Allen, the wealthy chief justice of Pennsylvania, to lobby for his appointment. Their influence worked; he was named to the postmastership with William Hunter, a Virginia printer, as his colleague. Their joint salary would come out of any profits from the postal revenues.

Now Franklin had not only the prestige of a royal official but also a government expense account to let him travel wherever he liked in the colonies. He set out at once to familiarize himself with the condition of the postal service. He made two long trips, first to all the post offices in the north, and then to those in Maryland and Virginia, bumping over the roads, crossing on the ferries, talking to the officials, checking their efficiency.

He observed the functioning of this social service as carefully as he studied nature. The result: practical improvements in the way everything was done. He turned casual accounting into a uniform system, furnishing all post offices with printed instructions and standardized forms. For the people he provided a more regular and frequent service: three times a week in spring and summer between Philadelphia and New York, instead of once, and twice a week between New England and Philadelphia. In the other seasons it would be twice weekly. He increased postal revenues so much that for the first time ever London drew a profit from the colonial service.

The Franklin family profited too, and by more than Ben's salary of £300 a year. He gave several of his relatives or friends appointments in the service, beginning with his son William, who replaced Franklin as Philadelphia's postmaster. Call it patronage or nepotism, it was as common two hundred years ago—or two thousand years ago—as it is now.

Franklin's experience in diplomacy began in 1753 when he was appointed to a Pennsylvania commission of three whites to deal with the Indians at a treaty session in Carlisle. Riding hard, it took four days over rough trails to reach the village. They arrived on September 26 and found about a hundred Indians representing the Six Nations of the Iroquois. With them the whites brought wagon loads of gifts—blankets, coats, shirts, cloth, guns, powder, lead, flints, knives, and rum.

Such conferences were not new. Since William Penn's day they had often been the scene of bargaining, for the lands the whites coveted were hardly empty. They belonged to a number of Indian tribes that did their best to resist the claims the English and the French made upon their lands. Franklin's group came instructed to renew and confirm the treaty of friendship made earlier. What the Indians wanted now was assurance there would be fewer white men crossing the mountains into their hunting grounds. They wanted fewer traders, fewer trading posts—and fewer kegs of rum. After four days of ceremony and talk, the commissioners agreed, hoping for peace on the frontier and for Indian allies against the French.

What Franklin wrote of these early contacts with the Indians indicates that his opinions were as racist as most of the white colonizers'. They saw the Native Americans through a European looking glass; the image was badly distorted. Unable to understand new and strange cultures, the whites called the Indians savages. To the Indians the land was for all, to be held in common. To the whites the land the Indians lived on was open territory to be grabbed at will.

In Franklin's early comments he spoke of the Indians as lazy, vain, mediocre people. He distrusted them and had no faith in negotiations for treaties. "I do not believe we shall ever have a firm peace with the Indians till we have well drubbed them," he wrote. But much later, after long personal experience, he came to admire the dignity with which they conducted themselves in negotiations and the vivid way they voiced their views. It angered him that these "savages" were so unfairly treated by the "civilized" whites. "Almost every war between the Indians and whites," he said, "has been occasioned by some injustice of the latter toward the former."

He did not believe the Indians could or would be assimilated into white culture. But why must the two peoples war against each other? With honest trading and fair treaties respected on both sides, couldn't they live peaceably? He thought there would always be a frontier where the Indians could continue their own way of life. And yet he believed at the same time that it was America's destiny to colonize the continent where Indians had lived for countless centuries before the white invasion.

There was one aspect of Indian life that Franklin believed whites had much to learn from. With his natural curiosity he had learned something about the groups of Indians in the northeast known together as the Iroquois. Most of them lived in villages ruled by chiefs. The men hunted and the women farmed. The women had a special role:

they not only controlled the land and the house, but they also chose the chiefs. In the past, bitter fighting among the tribes of that region had done great harm. To stop it, around the year 1400 the leaders of five tribes (a sixth was to be added later), in what is now central New York State, had formed the League of the Iroquois. They lived under a constitution that had three main principles: peace, equity or justice, and "the power of the good words"—that is, the wisdom of the elders. Meeting in council, the chiefs discussed threats of war and planned for a common defense. There had to be unanimous agreement for action to be taken.

Franklin admired this early model of a United Nations. The Indians themselves, ten years earlier, had suggested that the colonists form a nation like their own Iroquois Confederacy. At a meeting of the Pennsylvania legislature in 1744, an Onondaga named Canassatego had urged the idea upon the colonists. It seemed a good idea to many of the whites; they began studying examples of union: in the Bible, in the annals of classical Greece and Rome, and particularly in the experience of the Iroquois Confederacy.

Franklin obviously had it in mind when he began to think about the need for bringing the American colonies together in some sort of union that would advance their common interests:

It would be a strange thing if Six Nations of ignorant savages should be capable of forming a scheme for such union, and be able to execute it in such a manner as that it has subsisted ages and appears indissoluble, and yet a like union should be impracticable for ten or a dozen English colonies, to whom it is more necessary and must be more advantageous, and who cannot be supposed to want an equal understanding of their interests.

But how to bring about such united action? As he thought about strategy and tactics, he borrowed from the Iroquois the plan for an intercolonial council. The colonies would send delegates to it, with meetings rotating among their capitals, and a governor appointed by the Crown would chair the sessions. To fund the council he suggested a tax on hard liquor. He did not want the Crown to impose such a union. He would much prefer that the colonies create their own union. But with all the political differences among them, the economic rivalries, the prima donnas reluctant to give way to others, how could you get the colonies to see the need for union and find the means to achieve it?

As early as 1751 Franklin was setting down on paper his thoughts on the matter. In a letter to James Parker, his business partner in New York, he said he'd like to train half a dozen good men as unofficial ambassadors to visit all the colonies and convince their leading men to promote his scheme for an intercolonial union by pressing it both in private and in public. If objections were answered quickly, before they could take hold in the public mind, then such a union might be possible. Of course, it would take hard work and much time. But "a voluntary union entered into by the colonies themselves, I think, would be preferable to one imposed by Parliament; for it would be perhaps not much more difficult to procure, and more easy to alter and improve as circumstances should require and direct."

He created a visual image to dramatize the urgency of union when the Seven Years War between England and France began. Those powers had renewed their struggle for world dominion, and in 1754 the fighting spilled over into America. Here France and Britain contended for control of the Ohio Valley. That spring Virginia's governor sent twenty-one-year-old George Washington and a small military force to stop the French from building Fort Duquesne (near the site of today's Pittsburgh). But with the aid of Indian allies, the French drove Washington off. The French and Indian War, as it was called in America, had begun.

In his *Pennsylvania Gazette* for May 9, 1754, Franklin published a report on the French advance into the Ohio region. With it he printed a cartoon of a snake sliced into several sections labeled for each of the colonies. He captioned his cartoon, "Join, or Die." Other colonial papers quickly copied it.

Alarmed by the French advance, London called

Franklin's symbolic print,
warning the colonies to unite
against the common enemy

for a treaty with the Six Nations of the Iroquois
that would redress their grievances and keep them
from fighting for the French. To make a treaty
with the Indians and work out a plan of defense
against the French, the colonies sent delegates to a
meeting in Albany, New York.

The small town of Albany was the gateway to
Canada and close to the scene of conflict. Franklin
and the four other delegates from Pennsylvania
traveled overland to New York and then by sloop
up the Hudson to Albany. They carried not only
gifts for the Indians but also Ben's plan for an

intercolonial union. He did not want a temporary alliance just to defeat the French, which was all London desired. No, he saw Albany as the chance to win the colonies for a lasting confederacy, one that would work in peace as well as in war.

There was no thought of independence—not yet. He hoped only for a better and stronger connection among all the American colonies within the British Empire. It seemed so sensible to him, and why not to everyone else? For here was France, acting as a single force, commanded by one supreme authority, threatening Britain's hold on America. And yet the colonies still persisted in acting separately! Nevertheless, Franklin smelled union in the air. He had studied all the arguments against it, and he believed he had the answers.

While waiting five days for the last of the Indian chiefs to appear, the delegates met at the State House to talk. Franklin was the dominant figure, a man of world renown for his scientific achievements. Tall and strong, he dressed neatly and stylishly. When in formal session he wore a short wig, but otherwise his long brown hair came down to his shoulders. He looked little like the old frontiersman in the coonskin hat who would delight the French a quarter of a century later.

A delegate raised the main question for consideration: isn't a union of the colonies absolutely necessary for their security and defense? Ben's work: he had been busy lobbying for his union plan. By now several who were persuaded that a confederacy was a good idea helped him to convince other delegates that union would bring benefits to all the colonies. A motion was passed to appoint a committee of seven—Franklin among them, of course—to bring in a proposal. Out of his pocket came his "Short Hints" on a plan for uniting the colonies.

Meanwhile, as the committee set to work, there were negotiations with the Iroquois over purchase of their land. A land fever had swept the colonies. You couldn't get rich by going into manufacturing: British policy forbade such competition with their business. So investing in land was the only way to wealth. Everyone who had or could borrow money plunged into land speculation. Few remembered what the Quaker William Penn had once said: if whites wanted a peaceable community, they should not settle on land until it had been bought fairly from the Indians. But who had listened? In Franklin's colony, German and Scotch-Irish settlers by the thousands had moved west to squat on Indian lands. Though the enraged Indians burned their cabins and drove them off, it did not stem the tide. By now the Indians knew their hold on ancestral land was broken forever.

Days of dickering concluded with contracts for the sale of land. At the end, Tiyanoga, the Mohawk chief, spoke:

> We are ready to sell you this large tract of land for your people to live on. Yet after we

have sold our land, we in a little time have
nothing to show for it. But it is not so with
you. Your grandchildren will get something
from it as long as the world stands. Our
grandchildren . . . will say we were fools for
selling so much land for so small a matter,
and curse us. Therefore let it be a part of
the present agreement that we shall treat
one another as brethren to the latest generation, even after we shall not have left a
foot of land.

The whites agreed, but it was only words. They
soon forgot them. In the next days promises were
made to the Indians: restrictions on the sale of
liquor to them would be enforced. (They weren't.)
And questionable land deals would be looked into
and corrected. (How many were?)

Meanwhile, Franklin's committee discussed his
proposal for union. They enlarged and amended
it, then brought it into the full Albany Congress
for debate. There is no record of the arguments
made, but they are remembered as "energetic and
eloquent." Urgent, too, for the French danger
made everyone nervous. And though the colonies
"were extremely jealous of each other," Franklin
said, they managed to reach agreement.

At this time there was no thought of splitting
away from Britain. The delegates were proud of
their heritage. They saw a brilliant future for the
colonies, but not one separate from the Empire.

True, they might oppose some policies of the Crown, but wasn't that in the best British tradition of resistance to injustice or tyranny? It didn't mean they wanted to rebel against the mother country.

Franklin's Plan of Union, approved July 10, foreshadowed the federal organization of the states that would come years later. It called for a union of all the colonies under a president appointed and paid for by the Crown. A grand council elected by the colonial assemblies would have legislative power over Indian affairs, including new land purchases "not now within the bounds of particular colonies." Each colony would have from two to seven delegates, depending upon its contribution to the general treasury.

There was much dispute about the plan, but in the end the delegates agreed on it unanimously. The final form was not all Franklin had wished for, but, as he said, "When one has so many different people with different opinions to deal with in a new affair, one is obliged sometimes to give up some smaller points in order to obtain greater." The delegates took the plan home to lay before their assemblies. Copies were sent to the king and Parliament for their approval.

The result? Both the colonies and the British government rejected it. Not even Pennsylvania accepted it. Each colony had its reasons; none was ready to part with any bit of power that would be given to the general government. Franklin was ahead of his time. The plan was too new, too

radical. He was disgusted. Everybody cries out that
it's necessary, he said, but no one will accept it. If
there was ever to be a union, he thought, it would
have to be imposed upon the colonies by the king
and Parliament. And they too said no. They were
shocked by this brash attempt to create a government that would depend so little upon the Crown.
Note the contrast: the colonial assemblies rejected
the plan because they thought it gave the Crown
too much power, while the Crown thought it gave
the colonies too much power.

When your plan is so badly defeated, you might
understandably give it up. Not Franklin. He at
once set about figuring out how to reshape it, how
to take care of objections, how to win broader
support. His reaction was typical of his confident,
optimistic nature. Failure didn't crumble his will.
He didn't growl at his opponents, nor seek revenge.
He didn't waste time feeling sorry for himself. He
stayed cool, sent friends better versions of his idea,
and saw to it that those ideas reached the public.
He was a master of public relations, that is, of the
methods for promoting a project.

One of these methods was a series of letters he
sent to the Massachusetts governor, William Shirley.
The governor had proposed a variant of Franklin's
Plan for Union that would place even greater
authority in the hands of the Crown, giving Parliament all the power to tax the colonials. Franklin
asked Shirley if it was wise to separate a people
from their government. They bear the burdens of

citizenship better when they have some share in the direction, he said. "In matters of general concern to the people . . . it is of use to consider as well what they will be *apt* to think and say, as what they ought to think."

As for taxation, he went on, it was the undoubted right of Englishmen never to be taxed but by their own consent, given by their representatives. What Shirley and the Crown seemed to desire "shows a suspicion of their loyalty to the Crown, or regard for their country, or of their common sense and understanding, which they have not deserved. Compelling the colonies to pay money without their consent would be rather like raising contributions in an enemy's country, than taxing of Englishmen for their own public benefit. . . . It would be treating them as a conquered nation, and not as true British subjects."

Twenty years later, when the Revolution broke out, his ideas would be echoed again and again.

CHAPTER TEN

OUR MAN IN LONDON

Biographers have a good time speculating about Benjamin Franklin's emotional life. One calls him "a racy and roguish figure . . . who never lost his interest in women." Another says, "Emotionally starved by a marriage which was, at its best, peaceful, he energetically sought the affection of younger women." We know that he had an illegitimate son, and some flings in London when he worked there as a young printer. Now, nearly fifty, he met twenty-one-year-old Catharine Ray of Rhode Island while on a tour of post offices early in 1755. They traveled together part of the way, and visited her sister's home. He began to write her long letters that were both chatty and intimate. He would develop other such relationships with young women until well into his eighties.

His correspondence with Kathy, as he called her, lasted more than thirty years, through her marriage and his own wife's death, although he saw her only about four times during his life. In his first letter he told her, "Your favors come mixed with the snowy fleeces, which are pure as your virgin innocence, white as your lovely bosom, and— as cold."

A little later he wrote:

> . . . I hear you are now in Boston, gay and lovely as usual. Let me give you some fatherly advice . . . Kill no more pigeons than you can eat. Be a good girl and don't forget your catechism. Go constantly to meeting, or church, till you get a good husband, then stay at home, and nurse the children, and live like a Christian. Spend your spare hours in sober whisk, prayers, or learning to cipher. You must practice *addition* to your husband's estate, by industry and frugality; *subtraction* of all unnecessary expenses; *multiplication* (I would gladly have taught you that myself, but you thought it was time enough, and wouldn't learn), he will soon make you a mistress of it. As to *division*, I would say with brother Paul, let there be no division among ye. But as your good sister Hubbard (my love to her) is well acquainted with *the rule of two*, I hope you will become an expert in *the rule of three*, that when again I have the pleasure of seeing you, I may find you like my grapevine, surrounded with clusters,

plump, juicy, blushing, pretty little rogues, like their Mama. Adieu. The bell rings, and I must go among the grave ones, and talk politics.

Your affectionate friend,
B. Franklin

In another letter to Kathy he talks about his political and military doings, thanks her for a gift of excellent cheeses, and then adds:

> . . . Mrs. Franklin was very proud that a young lady should have so much regard for her old husband as to send him such a present. We talk of you every time it comes to table. She is sure you are a sensible girl, and a notable housewife, and talks of bequeathing me to you as a legacy; but I ought to wish you a better and hope she will live these hundred years; for we are grown old together, and if she has any faults I am so used to them that I don't perceive them. . . .

While he always found time for such friends, he didn't neglect his official duties. With the Albany plan vetoed, the colonies had no central scheme for defense against the French. In London, the government decided this was the time to capture Fort Duquesne and halt the French drive into the

Ohio Valley. Two regiments of British regulars were sent across the Atlantic to join with colonial forces. In March 1755 the British troops commanded by Major General Edward Braddock landed at Alexandria, Virginia. Braddock discovered that the colonial governors had failed to deliver the wagons and horses he needed to carry his army across Pennsylvania to the frontier. He turned to Franklin, the postmaster general, for help. In two weeks Franklin collected 150 wagons, with four horses to each wagon, and 259 saddle or pack horses, offering good prices. He pledged his own money for it (and was later repaid).

He found Braddock to be a cantankerous old man with little combat experience and an arrogant disdain for anyone else's opinion. Knowing what frontier conditions were like, Franklin tried to explain to Braddock the need for planning his attack for the way the French and Indians would be sure to fight. It would not be army against army on open fields of combat as in Europe. "He smiled at my ignorance," Franklin later wrote, and said, "These savages may indeed be a formidable enemy to your raw American militia, but upon the King's regular and disciplined troops, sir, it is impossible they should make any impression."

The general learned the hard way. His men met disaster on the Monongahela, eight miles from Fort Duquesne. Braddock was killed, and the victorious Indians swept into Pennsylvania ravaging the frontier. As the Indian attacks continued, Franklin proposed in the Assembly a bill to establish a voluntary militia. The pacifist Quakers were in the minority now, and the bill passed. When the governor vetoed it—partly because it provided that the officers be elected by the people, not chosen by the Crown—angry frontiersmen rode into Philadelphia and dumped a wagon load of scalped corpses on the steps of the State House. At once the Assembly voted a large sum of money for defense.

Franklin, with his son William as his guide, was sent out to determine how best to protect the threatened communities. His job was to raise troops, furnish arms, and build a line of forts. To organize a frontier people panicked by war took a powerful will, a quick and decisive mind, and the ability to get others to follow orders. Franklin had shown these talents before, but under very different circumstances. Yet he did his work well in the seven harsh weeks he spent on the frontier, commanding an army of 560 men, rebuilding forts, and erecting stockades. He marked his fiftieth birthday—January 17, 1756—shivering in the winter rain with his Pennsylvania militia.

Home in February, he was named colonel of the militia just recruited, a force of some twelve hundred men. Such official honors disgusted the Penns. What right had these colonials to elect their officers? They called Franklin "a dangerous man" and wished he would disappear. "However, as he

Colonel Franklin, mounted on horse in the center of his militia parade, is honored by the homefolk.

is a sort of Tribune of the People, he must be treated with regard," they said.

The battle with the proprietors never let up. Whatever the Assembly tried to do, the governor tried to block. When the English forces were broken by the French and Indians, the Assembly voted heavy taxes to improve defense. But even for this emergency the governor would not allow them to tax the Penn estates.

Sick of this opposition, the Assembly determined to go around the governor and take its case directly to the Crown. They decided to send Franklin to London as their special agent.

The office of colonial agent was not a new thing. Agents performed an important function from the earliest colonial times. Their job was to speak for the colony before the English governing bodies. They presented petitions and lobbied for their approval; they criticized old laws and proposed new ones when necessary; they promoted colonial trade and gave advice in boundary disputes; they were consulted on military, Indian, and financial affairs. Every colony had its man in London to promote the welfare of the people that sent him there. Policymakers both at home and in London used the agents as go-betweens. Their role became even more vital at the time of Franklin's appointment. For it was around then that decisions that would lead to the American Revolution began to take form.

As agent for Pennsylvania, Franklin's first object was to convince the king and his Privy Council that the proprietary estates should be taxed. His second was to suggest that the proprietorship be abolished and that the province be taken under the direct rule of the Crown. If the Penns could be taken off their back, the colonists believed that they would enjoy much greater freedom.

So the man who had last seen London as a journeyman printer would return as the agent of his colony. A poor workman when he left the Empire capital, he was now a rich and famous man of science. His prestige, of course, made him the right choice to be the colony's lobbyist. As the head of his party, his political talents were known to all. And he would need them to persuade London to do what the colony desired. It would not be an easy task. The agents of some of the other colonies were finding that British officials treated them disdainfully, like underlings.

When Franklin accepted the mission, he heard jeers as well as cheers. Not everyone in Philadelphia applauded his appointment. Many of the local aristocrats were not friendly to him—not so much because of his plain origins, but because of his strong opposition to the proprietary party. This was their party, the Tory party of the upper classes. They called him a hypocrite, charging that he wanted to go to London to serve himself, not the colony. A rumor spread that he would try to put the colony in the king's hands so he could have himself made governor.

News that Franklin had been chosen agent didn't worry Thomas Penn. "Mr. Franklin's popularity is nothing here," he wrote from London; "he will be looked upon very coldly by great people; there are very few of any consequence that have heard of his electrical experiments, those matters being attended to by a particular set of people. . . . But it is quite another sort of people who are to determine the dispute between us."

Franklin made out his will, providing for friends and twenty-two relatives. His parents were dead, and only one of his brothers was left. He arranged for the care of a half-sister, now seventy-nine. His youngest and favorite sister, Jane Mecom, forty-five, was the mother of nine. (He had trained her son Benjamin as a printer and set him up in business in Antigua.) Finally, in June 1757, Ben sailed from New York. With him was his son William, who would serve as his secretary and also study law at the Inns of Court in London. They took their two slaves, Peter and King, and left behind Deborah and thirteen-year-old Sally, their lively daughter. It was not too sad a farewell, for everyone expected Franklin to be gone only some months.

He looked forward eagerly to London. He wanted to do all he could for his colony—and yes, for himself, too. Accomplished as he was in so many other fields, his reputation would be enhanced by success in this new mission. He would represent only Pennsylvania: there was no American nation as yet, nor did anyone dream there ever would be. He spoke of going to England as going "home."

After twenty-seven days at sea, dodging French warships and nearly getting wrecked on the Scilly Islands, the packet reached England. There were quick visits to such old friends as Peter Collinson and William Strahan, and then the Franklins settled into their lodgings at 36 Craven Street. The three-story house, near Charing Cross, was small but comfortable. The Franklins had four furnished rooms on the second floor. It would be his home all during his stay. His landlady was a charming widow, Mrs. Margaret Stevenson, and she and her daughter Polly, warming at once to this genial, witty old man, treated him like one of the family. He enjoyed young Polly's company, and as he had with Catharine Ray back home, became her friend for life.

From his home on Craven Street, he could walk in a few minutes to Whitehall, the seat of government. He was close by Fleet Street too, the newspaper district thickly dotted with coffeehouses where politicians and gossips gathered to swap the news and argue the issues. His favorite was St. Paul's, where his best friends—scientists and writers of "Honest Whig" views—met every Thursday.

With some 750,000 inhabitants, the London of his day was the greatest city in Europe. Huge, but not healthy. The streets stank of sewage and garbage, the air was polluted with the smoke of coal fires, and the noise of the wheeled traffic, the shouts of peddlers, the songs of balladeers, assaulted the ear. Food rotted for lack of refrigeration, the water was too foul to drink, and the death rate was devastating. People swigged down so many millions of gallons of raw gin or wine that gout was the disease of choice. (Ben's own favorite drinks were rum and Madeira.)

From the countryside unskilled workers flooded into the city and kept wages so low—if you were

*The home of Mrs. Stevenson in London,
where Franklin took four furnished
rooms on the second floor*

lucky enough to find a job—that the earnings of a man who worked a whole week were barely enough to pay for a pound of tea. Poverty swarmed in the streets and alleys, and so did crime and prostitution. The most trivial offense could set you swinging on the gallows at Tyburn. No wonder that from time to time furious riots exploded.

But if you had money, there were pleasures aplenty. Bare-knuckle bouts drew big crowds, and cockfighting was just as popular. At the horse races elegant ladies and gentlemen displayed the exquisite new fashions. There were concerts and balls and theaters. Men belonged to fashionable clubs, where tens of thousands of pounds could be dropped in one night at the gaming table. Royalty, the titled, and the rich had their palaces, their town houses, their magnificent country homes, their parks and gardens designed by superb architects and landscape artists.

Although a few hundred of the nobility dominated British society, talented and energetic men of the middle class could rise to great influence. Business and trade became a path to power. Coal, tobacco, sugar, iron, the slave trade made many rich. Americans too could grab a rung on the ladder of enterprise and climb high. Many were as much at home in London as in Charleston or Boston or New York. Some Americans, who came and stayed, rose to knighthood or to a seat in Parliament. It was in that Anglo-American society that Franklin found a new home.

Early on, a friend introduced him to Lord Granville, head of the Privy Council. A brother-in-law of Thomas Penn, he still treated Franklin politely but advised him that his colony was very wrong to think that the king's instructions to the governor were not law and that the Assembly was free to accept or reject them. They are "the law of the land," he insisted, "for THE KING IS THE LEGISLATOR OF THE COLONIES." The shocked Franklin noted these words in capital letters. They made the Assembly's wishes worth nothing. He replied that this doctrine was new to him. He had always understood from the colony's charter that although the Assembly could not make law without the king's assent, neither could the king make law for the colony without its assent. "Totally mistaken!" said Granville.

This was a bad beginning for his mission. How could it be? He remembered that twenty years earlier, the House of Commons had thrown out a proposal by the Crown that its instructions must be law in the colonies. Well, he would see what he could do in tactful talks with the Penns. He met several times with the brothers Thomas and Richard, to little effect. Finally they asked him to state his case in writing. This he did, listing the Assembly's grievances, ending by saying that the exemption of the Penn estates from taxation appeared to the people to be "both unjust and cruel."

The Penns handed this paper to England's attorney general for an opinion. There it lay unanswered for a long year while Franklin pestered the Penns for a quick reply. Then, bypassing Franklin, the Penns wrote to the Assembly and advised it to send a more suitable agent to London.

The wrangling went on much longer. Clearly Franklin would not be able to reach a settlement soon. It came down to the Penns' denying that the colonists had the rights of Britons. After one set-to with the "insolent" Thomas Penn, Franklin wrote that he never felt for any man living a more thorough contempt. Cutting him off abruptly, the Penns refused to see him anymore; he could deal with them only through their lawyer.

The Penns vilified him in government circles, blackening his name, doubting his integrity. And this with the very people with whom he had to deal. The right connections were all-important if one would get things done in government. Although Franklin had lots of friends in England, they were not among the king's ministers or the policymakers.

He wanted the Privy Council to lay the proprietary issue before the House of Commons. They wouldn't, he said, because they feared the Parliament would establish too much freedom in the colonies; they didn't like the Commons to meddle in such affairs. Painfully, Franklin was learning how this bureaucracy worked. He had mistakenly assumed that men elected to the House were independent and public-spirited, and would understand the problems of British citizens in the colonies. He found out that mostly they did what the king's ministers asked.

He politicked, and waited, and politicked, and waited, but still had himself a great time. Biographers agree that these were probably the happiest years of his life. Now that he was a diplomat, he adorned himself with a new wig and bought two silver buckles. Happily he basked in the domestic warmth of Craven Street. Margaret Stevenson became much like a wife to him, though there is no evidence they ever shared a bed. Debby's letters from home, frequent and lively, told him whatever he wanted to know. But his replies were few. He warned her that he might not return for another twelve months, for he'd learned his mission "requires both time and patience." He missed his "domestic comfort and felt a longing desire" to be back with his family.

Yet pleasant company gave him little time to feel lonely. He dined out as much as he liked, was always welcome, and enjoyed the friendship of scientists and merchants. James Boswell, watching him play chess at a club, remarked that Franklin was "all jollity and pleasantry."

His friend William Strahan wrote a teasing letter to Deborah, urging her to pocket her fears of an ocean trip and come over to join her husband, "for who knows what repeated strong temptation may, in time, and while he is at so great a distance from you, accomplish." Yet she never came, nor did Franklin believe she would. Whether he did have affairs in these London years no one knows. If he did, he kept them quiet.

He sent off many presents to his family: damask tablecloths, carpets, gowns for Debby and Sally, china, silver, blankets, books, music, a gadget to core apples, a new kind of candlesnuffer. And even a big beer jug. "I fell in love with it at first sight," he wrote Debby, "for I thought it looked like a fat jolly dame, clean and tidy, with a neat blue and white calico gown on, good natured and lovely, and put me in mind of—somebody." Tenderly he chose special gifts for Debby. He sent her a large-print prayer book so she wouldn't have to use her spectacles in church, a screen to shield her eyes from the candle's flame, and a reading glass of silver and tortoiseshell. No longer the penny-pinching youth of his apprentice years, he was just as generous with gifts to friends back home.

Summers he and William went sightseeing. They spent many hours tracking down the Franklin line. In Ecton, the village where Franklin's father and many generations before him had lived, they found the ancestral home, now turned into a schoolhouse, and the graveyard where their slave Peter scraped the moss from the tombstones so William could copy the inscriptions. They made friends of surviving cousins and then went on to find some of Deborah's relatives near Birmingham, where they had a jolly time swapping family tales at the dinner table.

On a trip to Scotland, Ben was given the hon-

orary degree of Doctor of Laws from the University
of St. Andrews, and then another doctorate from
Oxford University. Now he would be "Dr. Franklin"
for the rest of his life. Edinburgh and Glasgow
welcomed him officially, and distinguished Scots
were added to the inner circle of his English friends.

Some of these new friends he visited at their
country homes for weeks at a time. Especially was
he welcome at Twyford in Hampshire, where his
warm friend Bishop Shipley lived. He was sought
out too by the diplomatic corps, who wanted to
hear of American affairs. Important to foreign
courts, he said, who "begin to hope Britain's alarm-
ing power will be diminished by the defection of
her colonies."

But as the years in England passed, his ties with
home weakened. Some friends said he forgot them
as soon as they were out of sight. Unlike Debby,
he could feel at home quickly in new places, sub-
stituting a new "family" for his own remote one.
As his letters home became fewer and shorter,
Debby, who had never been able to live anywhere
but nearby her childhood home, must have
suffered.

It took three years for Franklin's official business
to be settled. In 1760 the lawyers for both sides
worked out an agreement. The king approved the
Pennsylvania Assembly bill taxing the proprietary
estates at the same rate as comparable property
and exempting only their lands not yet surveyed.

His mission concluded, why didn't Franklin go

home? He stayed in London another two years. Had he begun to feel more and more English, and less and less American?

Perhaps. But one reason he stayed had to do with his son William. A charming young man, poised and polished, he had finished his legal studies and been admitted to the bar. He had gone everywhere with his father and entered easily into Franklin's intimate circle.

In October 1761 the Franklins rejoiced at the coronation of England's new king, twenty-two-year-old George III—"the very best in the world and the most amiable," Ben said. Affectionate as you Americans feel now, said an English friend, Charles Pratt, you'll one day want your independence. Americans have no such idea, he replied, nor will they ever, "unless you grossly abuse them." Very true, said Pratt, but it will happen!

Now in this thirties, William had to find his niche in the world. His father was regarded as the most important American by the mother country. The son counted on the father's influence in government. Those friends in positions of power no doubt wanted to solidify Franklin's allegiance to the Crown by giving his son a high appointment. In 1762 it all came together. William, thirty-one, was named the royal governor of the colony of New Jersey.

"A shameful affair," said the Penns of this appointment. Crusty John Adams didn't like it either. He called it "some kind of backstairs in-

William Franklin, first-born son,
from a crayon drawing

trigue" and "an insult to the morals of America,"
this "elevation of a base-born brat." Adams did not
know that in 1760 the "brat" had himself fathered
an illegitimate son, called William Temple Franklin.
Who the mother was, no one knows. But grandfather Ben took over the infant's care. William, late
in 1762, married Elizabeth Downes, the daughter
of a wealthy Barbados sugar planter.

With "extreme regret" Franklin sailed for America on August 23, 1762, and after ten weeks at sea reached Philadelphia. He found the family well and his house full of friends welcoming him with great affection. For years, while he was away, he had been reelected unanimously to the Assembly, disproving what enemies were saying about his loss of popularity. Yet he wrote his London friend Strahan that within two years he would be back in England if he could persuade Debby to cross the seas.

CHAPTER ELEVEN

RAIDS AND RIOTS

Homecoming was wonderful. But the feeling didn't last long. Franklin missed England. He marveled that such a tiny island could muster so much more brilliance and wit than his own vast America. Where was the poetry, the painting, the music that could match the genius of England? He hoped America would catch up when it mastered its struggle for the plain necessities of life.

In his own home, however, he found pleasure in a renewed closeness with his daughter Sally, now nineteen. They played duets, he on his newly invented harmonica, she on the harpsichord. Son William returned from London with his wife and took up his duties as governor of New Jersey. The newlyweds made their home in a luxurious mansion in Burlington, just twenty miles upriver from Philadelphia. (William had left his two-year-old son in England, to be cared for by Strahan.)

Franklin was soon back at his duties as assemblyman for Philadelphia and postmaster general of

all the colonies. For his years of service in England
the legislators voted him the generous sum of
£3,000 plus expenses. He plunged into work, active
on eleven committees preparing bills. The year
1763 started well for the colonies. The Treaty of
Paris was signed in February, ending the long war
between Britain and France, and placing all of
North America east of the Mississippi under the
British flag. The terms of the treaty gave all French
territory in Canada to England, while France got a
few small but valuable islands in the Caribbean.

Franklin set out to improve the postal service
he had been out of touch with for years. When
spring came, he began a series of inspection tours
to the upper colonies. He wanted to speed up the
mail by making it operate by night as well as by
day, and to connect the delivery system with Mon-
treal and Quebec. He spent a month in Virginia,
then asked Debby to join him on a New England
tour. As usual, she wouldn't leave home, so he rode
off with Sally for company. They visited William in
New Jersey and then went on to New York and
Rhode Island, where he saw Catharine Ray (now
Mrs. Greene, with two daughters) for the first time
in eight years.

In his hometown of Boston no one was left of
his big family but Jane Mecom. He stayed with her
all summer while Sally was put up at a cousin's. At
fifteen Jane had married an illiterate saddler and
borne him twelve children; she would outlive all
but one. She was a vital, intelligent woman who

*As colonial postmaster, Franklin traveled widely
to develop improvements in the delivery system.*

drew great joy from her brother Ben. Giving her
far more than a constant shower of gifts, he treated
her gently and lovingly. Poor Debby, however, who
had waited over five years for her husband's return
from abroad, now waited another seven months
for him to complete his eighteen-hundred-mile tour
of the colonies.

Though officially peace had come, the frontier
was still an issue. Settlers and speculators had
thought that with the war over they could head
west to build an American empire. But London

ruled that the Americans were not to move into this new land. The colonists must stay where they were, on the seaboard. Why? Because the war had run up huge bills for Britain, and the government refused to add to those bills by protecting the colonists from the Indians on the frontier. That decision angered many Americans. Weren't they in the best position to determine what was good for the colonies? Why should some remote authority dictate what they could do on this side of the Atlantic?

But Britain insisted. Colonists west of a line of settlement were ordered out. It was too late. About 200,000 Indians lived between the Appalachian Mountains and the Mississippi River, a region then part of the British Empire. The French had told the Indians that the English would soon rob them of their hunting grounds. In the spring of 1763 several tribes, led by Chief Pontiac, rose in rebellion. By June they captured most of the British forts west of the mountains and killed many settlers. In desperation the British sent the Indian blankets infected with smallpox and used dogs to hunt them down. Many Indians died of disease or were killed in combat, but not until 1766 did Pontiac give up.

Franklin had urged that new colonies be planted by Britain in the western territory. He argued it would make the land safer by separating the Indians on one side from those on the other. He blamed the Pontiac uprising on the policy of refusing to supply the Indians with presents, ammunition, and rum, though he knew the constant inroads made by settlers was a greater cause.

On the far reaches of Pennsylvania, Scotch-Irish settlers had taken over lands not rightfully theirs. When they heard of the Indian outbreak, against which they had few defenses, they became so enraged they made victims of the innocent. A group called the Paxton Boys attacked a small village of peaceful Christian Indians at Conestoga and killed six of them. Two weeks later they raided the workhouse at Lancaster and murdered the fourteen Indians who had taken refuge there. British troops stationed nearby did nothing to save the Indians. The horrified Franklin wrote that "the spirit of killing all Indians, friend and foe, spread amazingly through the whole country."

The Assembly ordered the Paxton Boys to be arrested and tried. But the rioters, swelled now to over three hundred men, took the law into their own hands. They marched east toward Philadelphia to destroy 140 converted Indians who had been brought in for protection, and threatened to kill prominent Quakers whom they accused of inciting the Indians against the settlers. As they neared the city, the panicky governor appealed to Franklin for help. Franklin's advice was to stand firm. He quickly rallied troops and artillery to defend the city and went out with a small delegation to meet the mob at Germantown. We are prepared to defend the city, he told them, and there will be bloodshed if

*Indians massacred by the Paxton Boys in their raid
upon the workhouse at Lancaster in 1763.*

you move ahead. The leaders of the mob decided to turn back after demanding that their grievances be attended to. They wanted better defense for the frontier and fairer representation in the Assembly.

Franklin wrote one of his most eloquent manifestos against the brutal murderers: his "Narrative of the Late Massacre in Lancaster County." Yet he himself had urged the use of force against Indians. With the Paxton Boys back in their homes, no one, including Franklin, did anything to redress their grievances. He did not show much interest in the question of equality of representation. That idea was not yet a widely accepted principle anywhere in the British Empire. Even Pennsylvania had a more democratic system of representation than did the House of Commons.

In the Assembly, Franklin continued his battle with the Penns. He put the issue as province versus proprietary and continued to campaign for a change to royal government. He seemed to think that under the Crown the bitter conflicts within the colony would be easily resolved, and all would be peaceful again. But many feared the royal hand would rule the colony far more rigidly than the Penns. Would the colony be in danger of losing its valuable privileges? Would the Church of England restrict the religious liberty the colony had enjoyed ever since William Penn? Still the petition Franklin drafted to have the king take control from the Penns was adopted by the Assembly.

As the election of October 1764 approached, a

war of pamphlets broke out. Franklin made many enemies and was the target of their attacks, often focused on his personal life and his family: he came from the lowest class; his son was a bastard; he had passed off another's experiments as his own; he had pleasured himself in London at the colony's expense; he had taken bribes; he was two-faced; he had mishandled public funds. Although it was one of the nastiest campaigns in the colonies, some of the arguments against Franklin's policies were reasonable. In the end, his party won the election, but he was defeated—by a margin of only twenty-five votes out of four thousand cast.

Despite his defeat, the new Assembly voted to send him back to London as the colony's agent to petition the Crown for a change of government. This time, however, not unanimously; the vote was 19 to 11. He was hurt by his defeat; he suffered badly under the storm of invective unleashed by his opponents. He had worse enemies here at home, he felt, than in London.

It was a miserable time for him. He and Debby had begun the building of a new brick house on the south side of Market Street. But did he have a place there any longer? He had alienated so many people—the frontiersmen, the Germans, the Quakers, the proprietors' supporters—that his ability to lead the colony was gone. No longer would he be looked to as the great conciliator. Yet by nature, by temperament, he was born to that role. How well would he play the part in London this time?

CHAPTER TWELVE

A BRILLIANT PERFORMANCE

Early in November 1764, Franklin sailed for England. Hundreds of his admirers saw him off, and cannon roared a salute as he went on board the ship. (It would be ten years before he returned home, to a country priming its guns for revolution.) This time he traveled alone. His daughter Sally had hoped it would be her turn to accompany Papa, but he said her duty was to master her bookkeeping and take care of Mama. He reached London thirty days later and settled comfortably again into Margaret Stevenson's home on Craven Street.

It was a moment that marked the beginning of a great change in the relations between Britain and the colonies. With the British victory over the French, the colonists felt safe from the French threat and less worried about what the Indians might do along the frontier. Although they took pride in being a part of the Empire, they wanted to shape their own lives without depending upon the British.

But Britain was not thinking the same way. Rather than loosen control over the colonies, it wanted to solidify the Empire. Now, with a century of wars behind it, the government had time to pay closer attention to the colonies. And it needed to, for those wars had almost drained the treasury dry. The government had to find ways to pay its huge bills.

The Crown reasoned that the colonies had greatly benefited by Britain's defeat of France. Then why shouldn't the Americans pay a fair share of the costs of maintaining peace on the high seas and on the frontier? So in 1764 an act taxing sugar—and coffee and imported wines as well— was adopted to raise revenues in America.

Soon after, the British devised another way of raising money. It would lay a tax on many everyday things used in the colonies: newspapers, magazines, calendars, receipts, contracts, land titles, marriage licenses, wills, almanacs, ship's paper, insurance policies, even playing cards and dice. Stamps would be specially printed, and you'd buy and affix them to show you had paid the tax.

The idea was not new. The English had long paid such a tax. Before Franklin left Philadelphia, he had heard of the plan to raise money this way. It had not surprised him. He knew about the huge war debts and that Britain's civil and military costs in America were multiplying. The proposal did not alarm him. He urged only that the burden not be made too heavy.

To forestall criticism, Britain said money raised by the stamp tax would not flow to England. It would remain in the colonies to pay for British soldiers stationed there to protect the Americans. This isn't so bad, Franklin thought. If it works, fine. He didn't see Britain's and America's interests as separate and conflicting, but as part of one whole—the Empire. Why couldn't all parts prosper together? When the tax was voted in March 1765, Parliament provided that it not go into effect until November. The cautious government wanted to see how the colonies would react.

By the time Franklin left for London, he saw that the colonists wanted no part of the new tax. It had come on top of other unpopular acts by the king's ministers. There had been the Proclamation of 1763 preventing the colonists from settling west of the Appalachians. And then the Sugar Act, which the Americans were avoiding by wholesale smuggling. Was Britain trying to ruin colonial trade? And why couldn't Americans settle where they liked out west? And wasn't this Stamp Tax illegal? What voice did the Americans have in a government that did these things?

Part of the trouble came from disagreement over the meaning of representation in government. In England, people elected to Parliament were considered to represent not a particular city or

One of the Crown's stamps, alongside
an American propaganda stamp picturing
death as the outcome of the Stamp Act

county or district, but all the people of the Empire.
In the colonies, however, another view had developed. The people who lived in a particular place
chose a candidate to represent the needs and
interests of the people who lived in that place. So
when Parliament claimed that its members could
speak for all the colonies as well as Britain itself,
the Americans didn't see it that way. No Americans
sat in the House of Commons, nor could they, so
remote were they from London. Then how could
Parliament adopt a Stamp Act to tax the Americans
without their consent? Which is why Patrick Henry
spoke for the Americans when he shouted out in

the Virginia legislature that "Taxation without representation is tyranny!"

Massachusetts too denounced taxation without representation and called on the other colonies to write in protest. The legislature approved a Committee of Correspondence to contact the other colonies. Let's do without English lace and ruffles, said Boston's merchants, and the town's mechanics followed, refusing to wear leather work clothes made in Britain. By the end of 1764 the new weapon—refusing to use imported products—had spread to other colonies.

In London, Franklin hoped to convince the government that some other form of revenue-raising might be more palatable to the Americans. He lobbied long and hard against the tax measure, but when the government decided to have Americans administer it, he suggested that his friend, John Hughes, be appointed the agent for Pennsylvania. Such cooperation with the ministry was a bad mistake. He had figured the appointment would do a friend a favor and be of political advantage to himself, but it made it look as though he supported the Crown's tax policy.

In Boston, crowds rushed into the streets to hang the stamp officer in effigy and wreck his house. Violence spread through the colonies, and stamp officers hastily quit their jobs and fled. How could Franklin have been so slow to sense the depth of feeling back home? Perhaps because the habit of compromise was so ingrained. While he spoke out

Labelled a "Tory's Day of Judgment,"
this cartoon depicts the Crown's
stamp officer assaulted by patriots.

in London for American rights, he wrote letters to American friends deploring the violent mobs and their "blind leaders." He believed that kind of protest would only cripple the fight for repeal of the Stamp Act. "A firm loyalty to the Crown," he said, "will always be the wisest course to take."

His tightrope act gave Ben's enemies the opening to charge him with helping to put through the Stamp Act in the hope of being appointed governor of Pennsylvania. Friends wrote that his life would not be safe if he were caught in Philadelphia. One September night mobs threatened both John Hughes's house and Franklin's. Deborah, refusing to flee, bravely stood guard at home armed with a borrowed gun. The rioters were turned back by eight hundred citizens who came out on the streets to see that the peace was kept.

Believing it as hopeless to kill the Stamp Act as to stop the sun from setting, Franklin turned to the mission for which he had been sent to London. He presented Pennsylvania's petition for a change from the proprietary to royal government. The Privy Council simply postponed action "for the present"—which really meant, forever. But Ben fooled himself into believing he'd win his case some day. He still saw the king as angel and Parliament as the devil. It was in the same light that he viewed the Stamp Act. It was Parliament's doing, not the king's, and therefore he hoped the king would force its withdrawal. Few Americans clung to that idea as long as Franklin. (Not until blood was spilled at the battle of Lexington would he change his mind.)

He seemed blind to the deeper significance of the resistance rising at home. Perhaps he was living too comfortably, indulging himself in the pleasures of London. Most of his friends, like himself, were well-to-do and tended to be conservative. Conservatives detested disorder and were always ready to compromise for the sake of peace and quiet.

So it was hard for Franklin to believe the news he got from home. Passions boiled so high that it was unsafe to say anything contrary to mass opinion. Even people of the middle and upper classes, hurt by Britain's recent measures, were joining in the protest movement. The Sons of Liberty—merchants, artisans, writers—were organizing resistance groups in the towns. Their network could swing the popular mood of protest into forceful action. Well before Franklin did, these patriots saw the issue as more than a small matter of taxes. It was becoming the far more important question: what kind of America do we the people want to create?

In October, the Stamp Act Congress met in New York, united on the principle of no taxation without representation. Delegates from nine colonies petitioned Britain to repeal the act. They published a Declaration of Rights and Grievances denying that Parliament had the right to tax the colonies.

Franklin no longer delayed. He got the signal

and plunged into the fight to repeal, using every weapon in the arsenal of political action: petitions, letters to the press, meetings with key government figures. He rallied support from British merchants and manufacturers hurt by the American ban on importations. He was astonishing in his energy and devotion. He collared members of Parliament, one after another, stressing the importance of the dispute, stating the case clearly, answering objections, correcting wrong impressions, filling in the ignorant.

He didn't forget the vast public outside the windows of Whitehall. His greatest skill was his power to persuade. He took up his pen to educate the English on the issues. In those days political pamphleteers rarely signed their work; they used pen names. A good thing for him, who didn't want to risk his royal appointment as postmaster. Besides, arguments from a colonial agent would have been suspect. Better if the words came from a less biased pen. He used humor, irony, sarcasm, but always appealed to reason. Since his name was not on his writing, enemies back home asked why he was silent, why he was not doing his job. But the majority knew better, and that fall Pennsylvania voted to keep him on as the colony agent.

Stronger than theories of representation or appeals to good sense was economic self-interest. A coalition of British and West Indies merchants formed to back the American case. The businessmen feared losing their profits if American resistance to buying their goods continued. The government heard from merchants in two dozen major cities urging the repeal of the Stamp Act. Finally, late in January 1766, hearings on the issue began in the House of Commons. About thirty witnesses were heard during those two weeks.

The petition from the Stamp Act Congress was presented to the House, but they refused to hear it. Members felt that by meeting in New York the nine colonies had committed an act of rebellion. Only the Crown could authorize such an assembly. The debate went on, often for twelve hours running. Some called the new philosophy of colonial rights a dangerous idea and said the distinction the Americans drew between king and Parliament was ridiculous. The Stamp Act was the decision of both king and Commons. William Blackstone, the great lawyer, told the House that "the colonies are dependent upon us, and if they attempt to shake off our dependence, we shall I hope have firmness enough to make them obey."

Franklin heard much of the debate as he sat waiting for his turn to testify. Finally, he was called, and stepped forward, dressed plainly, wearing a powdered short wig, looking composed and quietly self-confident. The House knew his worldwide reputation, and many members were among his friends. The clerk of the Commons spoke, asking his name and residence:

"Franklin, of Philadelphia."

It was the opening line of a great political drama,

with Ben as the leading character, and in a sense the director and producer too. Knowing he was no orator, he avoided making long speeches. Instead, he had carefully planted questions among friends of the American cause and rehearsed his answers. The questions were designed to let him spell out the American position in clear, brief, logical sequence, anticipating everything the opposition might raise. His answers to the 174 questions—and there were unfriendly ones too—showed a tremendous grasp of information and a mastery of language. His manner was always calm and reasonable. The examination—it lasted four hours as he stood on his feet—was published not only in English but also in French and German. His case was based on constitutional claims, but he also demonstrated that the stamp tax was not practical and could cost Britain the loyalty of the colonies.

It was a brilliant performance on the political stage, Franklin at his best. Few others could have stood up so well to such an ordeal. In February, by a vote of 275 to 167, the Stamp Act was repealed. Although it was the pressure of the British merchants that counted most in the repeal, there is no doubt that Franklin's lobbying and testimony greatly helped. He had championed America's cause and won a great victory. His reputation was restored. When the news reached home, toasts were drunk in honor of the hero of the hour. Who could criticize him now? In 1768 Georgia made him its agent, and soon after so did New Jersey and

Massachusetts. In London it was Ben Franklin who spoke for all America.

Although the Stamp Act was repealed, Parliament still insisted on its right to legislate for the colonies "in all cases whatsoever." There was even talk of demanding that the colonies pay for the expense of printing all those stamps the Americans had refused to take. With pointed humor Ben replied to the threat in a letter to a London newspaper. He said it reminded him of the Frenchman who used to stop Englishmen crossing the Pont Neuf, "with many compliments, and a red-hot iron in his hand. Pray, Monsieur, says he. Do me the favor to let me have the honor of thrusting this hot iron into your backside? Zoons, what does the fellow mean! Begone with your iron or I'll break your head! Nay, Monsieur, replies he, if you do not choose it, I will not insist upon it. But at least, you will in justice have the goodness to pay me something for the heating of the iron."

Franklin still hoped he could help bring about a peaceful solution of the conflict with Britain. He persisted in trying to convince influential Britishers to accept a union in which the colonies would be permitted to run their own internal affairs, subject to the king, of course, but with fair and equal representation in Parliament. In a letter to his friend Lord Kames, he outlined the proposal and then, reflecting his fading optimism, warned that the immense and fruitful territory of America would soon become a great and powerful country, "able to shake off any shackle that may be imposed upon her, and perhaps place them on the imposers."

Franklin's confidence in obtaining justice from Parliament faded rapidly. In a letter home to his old friend Joseph Galloway, he commented on the farcical performance of the Commons in many issues, blaming it on bribery and corruption. In George the Third's time, only three Englishmen in a hundred had the right to vote. So it took but a few votes to put a man in the Commons, and thus majorities were easily shaped. The power lay with the king and the landed aristocracy. By corrupt practices they manipulated elections. To reach the Commons, a candidate normally paid off the voters by as much as £4,000. When a reformer tried to get a bill passed in the House obliging new members to swear they had not paid bribes for votes, the House laughed him down. Everyone knew of the practice, and few were ashamed of it.

In these years Franklin often voiced opinions on government and law that made great sense then, and still do. He wrote that sometimes the British put "national honor" above justice when it acted. It feared to be considered weak by other nations if it repealed laws that it acknowledged were wrong. But "government is not established merely by power," he said; "there must be maintained a general opinion of its wisdom and justice, to make it firm and durable."

With the British government maintaining that it had "supreme authority" over the colonies, and the Americans insisting on their "rights," a conflict over basic principle was slowly heading for a passionate climax. As agent for the colonies, Franklin tried to find ways to diminish quarrels and conciliate differences. He took every opening to discuss issues with British leaders and continued to write frequently for the press. During his ten-year stay in London, he wrote some 125 articles and many pamphlets. He tried to see both sides, the better to seek compromise. But with all his skills as diplomat and propagandist, he had less and less influence in London. By 1768 no one who sympathized with the American cause was in office. He began to lose interest in lobbying and paid more attention to his own affairs. Even when the British stationed troops in Boston in 1768, he did not protest vigorously. His thoughts turned to home, to science, to travel on the continent.

CHAPTER THIRTEEN

A BOOK ABOUT HIMSELF

Trying to get anything done for the colonies was not easy. Franklin had to work his way slowly and painfully through a maze of bureaucratic agencies. For no one single department was in charge of relations with America. Speedy handling of a question was impossible. And if a decision was finally reached, it took many weeks for it to cross the Atlantic and many more for a reply to come back.

Franklin was the man in the middle of this morass. And after years of meeting with delay and confusion and indifference, he got tired of it. As power in London shifted from one minister to another in a constant game of musical chairs, he never knew whether his cause would be advanced or discarded. Writing to his son William, he said, "I am myself grown so old [he was sixty-two] as to feel much less than formerly the spur of ambition; and if it were not for the flattering expectation that by being fixed here I might more effectually serve my country, I should certainly determine for retirement without a moment's hesitation."

He had had rather more than his share of "public bustle" and looked forward to spending the rest of his days in private life. But not quite yet, not while he could still hope to be useful to the colonies. Meanwhile, as the years passed, Debby sat at home waiting for his return. His Philadelphia income went largely to her support. He lived abroad on his £300 a year from the post office, £500 as the Pennsylvania agent, £400 from Massachusetts, £100 from New Jersey, and another £100 from Georgia. But these salaries were often long delayed. Georgia was years in arrears. And because the royal governor of Massachusetts had not consented to Ben's appointment, he refused to send him a penny.

Soon after Franklin's departure, Debby had suffered a stroke that damaged her memory. He arranged for his sister Jane Mecom and her husband to live with her. Although Franklin thought Debby had enough income to live comfortably, she kept running up bills and borrowing money from friends. His letters advised her to be more careful with money and let him know if she needed more. "I am very low speretted . . . so very lonely," she wrote as her health worsened. He sent her gifts, but his brief and infrequent letters no longer brimmed with chatty news, and they did little to comfort her in her last years. Nor could she believe him when he kept saying he would return soon.

To make it worse, while away on the Continent, he had Margaret Stevenson write Debby to relay the news in his letters to her. And when he did write Debby, he told her Mrs. Stevenson was "the best woman in England."

In 1767, Franklin's daughter Sally married Richard Bache, an English merchant who had migrated to America after Franklin left. Franklin's partnership with David Hall had run out the year before, which meant a considerable cut in income. So he had advised Debby to arrange a frugal wedding and to give Sally a dowry of £500. He feared the Crown might remove him as postmaster at any moment, leaving Debby only the rental income from half a dozen houses he owned. The new Franklin house in Philadelphia was still not finished, and his letters instructed Debby on precisely how he wanted the rooms decorated.

He felt responsible for his enlarged family—brothers, sisters, nephews, nieces, cousins—even at the distance of thousands of miles and years of absence. As for his grandchildren, he would always take a hand in their education and careers. When William's illegitimate son Temple was sent to school in England, his grandfather kept a close watch on him. The teenager spent much time with Franklin in Craven Street. Franklin thought the boy not only intelligent but also "pleasing, sensible, manly," capable of making an expert lawyer. He urged William to direct him on that path so that he would grow up to be more than "a mere gentleman." And

Franklin's daughter, Sarah Bache,
painted by John Hoppner

when his sister Jane Mecom's grandchildren—Josiah and Jonathan Williams—came from Boston, he guided them into the London world.

As the 1770s opened, son William had been governor of New Jersey for many years, and daughter Sally had begun to raise her seven children, the first of whom she named Benjamin Franklin Bache. Both William and Sally had to be helped financially by their father. William had learned to be an elegant snob in his London years but couldn't support himself in the aristocratic style he aspired to. Sally's husband was hard up because of business reversals.

This was an era when children were expected to heed the advice of their parents, and Franklin was ready to unreel that advice by the yard. He had proved himself a great success, and his formula for achieving it—hard work, thrift, self-reliance— threaded his letters to his children. He could even write William pages about the need to exercise, and what form it should take, and how long it should last. But by this time father and son were drifting apart. Once his father's right arm, William now aligned himself with the Crown, not the colonists. As the conflicting political views of both hardened, Franklin's love for his son gave way, and he would later cut off all communication with him.

Whatever his personal and political concerns, Franklin always found time for young people. He wrote charming verses for Polly Stevenson on her birthday. When travel took him away from Craven Street, he sent her long, intimately detailed letters about his adventures and observations abroad. He felt part of the family at the house of Bishop Shipley at Twyford. The bishop and his lady had five daughters, the youngest of whom, Kitty, he was especially fond of. When she was eleven, he took her by carriage back to her school in London and reported to her mother Kitty's delightful analysis of her sisters' marriage prospects.

He spent many happy hours with a wide circle of friends, making the rounds of the London taverns and coffeehouses. He loved to eat and drink and of course to talk. "Wherever he went," writes his biographer, Esmond Wright, "Franklin attracted the questioning, dissenting, and scientifically curious. It was to plain folk with stimulating minds that he responded. . . . He was never of the Establishment. . . . Franklin made hardly any close or friendly contact with any peers. He was rarely entertained at the great houses, and, it seems, never inside the clubs. Neither by rank nor wealth was he of the elect in an England where the oligarchs ruled."

He made several trips across the English Channel during his long years in London. In 1766, with the queen's physician, his friend Sir John Pringle, he spent two months in Germany, and in 1767 and 1769 visited France, where he was presented to King Louis XV and his queen at Versailles. France was interested in him as a leader of the rebellious American colonies, which it would like to see break away and weaken the powerful British Empire. Ben wrote Polly Stevenson that he found at Versailles and Paris "a prodigious mixture of magnificence and negligence, with every kind of elegance except that of cleanliness and what we call tidiness."

Inching toward seventy, Franklin could waver between moods of serenity and bouts of despon-

As colonial agent in London, Franklin sat for his portrait by David Martin in 1767.

dency. In 1772 he wrote William that "I grow homesick, and being now in my 67th year, I begin to apprehend some infirmity of age may attack me, and make my return impracticable. I have also some important affairs to settle before my death, a period I ought now to think cannot be far distant."

Some six months later he believed that with a new minister in office America's prospects might improve. Now he felt better and let William see how happy he was. He wrote that he had many friends among the learned men and a fine reputation that protected him from snide attacks. He was so popular he could spend the whole summer in country houses of friends if he chose. Scientists coming from abroad made a point of visiting him, as did foreign ambassadors who wanted his judgment of the volatile mood in the colonies.

It was Franklin's interpretation—or manipulation—of that mood that greatly concerned the British government. He and William discovered that their letters were being secretly intercepted, opened, read, sealed again, and sent on their way. It was a form of espionage he got used to.

His "learned friends" sometimes sought his opinion. Joseph Priestley, the famous chemist, when invited to take a new post as librarian to an earl, asked for Franklin's advice. He replied that he couldn't tell him *what* to decide, but could tell him *how*. His letter describes his own method of writing down reasons for and against a choice in two columns labeled Pro and Con, then estimating their relative weights, separately and comparatively. When it all lies before you on the paper, you can judge better, he said, and are less likely to take a rash step. He called this system "prudential algebra."

Another of his friends, the Scottish economist, Adam Smith, submitted to Franklin each chapter of his *Wealth of Nations* as he wrote it, asking for criticism and suggestions.

Franklin's interest in science never lapsed, though he gave less time to experiment now. His curiosity was insatiable. In a letter to Debby about a summer trip out of London, he tells of going deep down into a coal mine near the coast, till "I was 80 fathoms under the surface of the sea which rolled over our heads; so that I have been nearer to both her upper and lower regions than ever in my life before."

In a letter to a French friend, he discusses the nature of death and the possibility of restoration to life. He told of three flies drowned in Madeira wine when it was bottled in Virginia and sent to London. When the bottle was opened in Franklin's presence and the wine poured, three flies fell into the glass. He strained them out of the wine and exposed them to the sun on a sieve. In three hours two of the flies began to wriggle, struggled up on their legs, dried their eyes, beat their wings and flew off, finding themselves in a strange land thousands of miles from where they started. He remarked that when it would come time for him to go, he wished he could be immersed in a cask of Madeira, then recalled to life in the same way, but a hundred years later, for he had an ardent desire to see what America would be like a century from now.

It was in 1771 that Franklin began to write his most influential work, the *Autobiography*. It was summer, and he was the family guest of the Shipleys in the tiny village of Twyford. Putting the intrigues of London behind him, he sat in his room to tell the story of the boy he had once been.

He wrote the book because, like most memoirists, it satisfied his vanity. And why not? Though people dislike vanity in others, they have a fair share of it themselves. He thought vanity one of the "comforts of life." In his case, it was justified, for few have lived so useful a life. Then, too, it was another way for him to give advice to the young. He had "made it" and wanted to show others how to do it. So he began the book in the form of a letter to his son William. It may have meant more than that. Perhaps, as the ties between father and son unraveled, Franklin hoped the book might draw them closer again.

Public pressures forced him to lay aside the book when it had brought him only to the year 1731, and the age of twenty-five. He did not pick it up again until thirteen years later, in France, and added more pages in Philadelphia in 1788. But he never finished it. It carries the story to 1765, when he still had nearly two decades more of life ahead.

Writing one's personal history in that time was much different from what it would become. There was no soul-searching, no tormented confession, no exposure of his own and others' sins and weaknesses. It was in part a do-it-yourself manual on how to get on in the world in the mode of his time. He could write about himself, says the historian Pauline Maier, "only by making himself into a cause, a model to show younger Americans how personal ambition and public service could be reconciled."

When he abandoned the *Autobiography* for a time, a friend who had read the first part urged him to continue it: You show that a man need not be ashamed of the origins from which he rose; he can be responsible for his own success. As in the epitaph he composed for himself at the age of twenty-two (see page 272), Franklin saw his life as a book authored by his own hand, and in the *Autobiography* this printer tells us what missteps he had made, what "errata" needed correction. His career was not shaped by God or king or aristocracy, but by himself. So it is that he teaches the reader how to create character, how to mold a public self. The *Autobiography* shows Ben consciously gathering the materials that will be forged into the figure of international fame.

All the evidence indicates that he was a very rapid writer. He wrote the first part of the *Autobiography* in less than two weeks "in the quiet retirement of Twyford, where my only business was a little scribbling." Out of that "scribbling" came one of the world's best-known books. He tells his story in a quiet and homely manner. The book is short and unemotional. It has many omissions: it does not give the full story of his marriage, his daughter Sally is ignored, and his son William is mentioned only in passing. Debby is included mostly for the time before they were married. He concentrates on himself, or that part of himself he wants the reader to see. He doesn't create any aura of glamour; no need to, for when he wrote, almost everyone knew who he was and what he had achieved. Kenneth Silverman, an editor of his work, points out that he "wrote from the point of view of his own legend. He would show his readers how he became what he knew he had in their minds become."

CHAPTER FOURTEEN

RESISTANCE MOVES TO REVOLUTION

While Franklin was writing his life story and enjoying London, a storm was gathering across the Atlantic. Once the Stamp Act was repealed, Parliament sought more revenue by placing heavier taxes on England's landed gentry. When they made a great uproar, Parliament took aim again at the colonies and passed the Townshend Acts, an even tougher tax program. It imposed import duties on America to be collected by Crown officials.

The news launched a new round of colonial protests. Again the Americans boycotted British goods. Massachusetts called on the other colonies to unite against the taxes, and for the reason given before: no taxation without representation! As the conflict intensified, the Americans began to split into two groups: the Patriots, who didn't fear a break with the British Empire, and the Loyalists or Tories, who remained faithful to the Crown.

Popular anger against British policy pushed

resistance toward revolution. The militant Sons of Liberty refused to let the Crown toy with their rights. Crowds captured and destroyed British customs vessels, forced officials to resign, tore down a governor's mansion, jeered at British soldiers. Loyalists who disapproved of such actions were scared to oppose them publicly. The Patriots tolerated little dissent by Tories; they would wreck their property, tar and feather them, drive them out of town. In Boston, on March 5, 1770, a crowd led by the Sons of Liberty gathered to confront British soldiers guarding the customhouse. Someone threw snowballs, the soldiers panicked, and shots were fired, killing five Americans and wounding several others. This was the Boston Massacre, used by the radicals as a chilling example of the British threat to liberty and the danger of a standing army in peacetime.

The alarmed Parliament backed down and in April removed the Townshend duties on everything but tea. They left that tax to let the colonies know the British had the right to pass such laws. Tension relaxed, and a period of relative calm followed for the next three years. During this time Franklin continued to believe that nonviolent protest was the way to gain what the colonists wanted. Yet he realized that the Crown's policy and the American resistance to it were sowing the seeds of a "total disunion of the two countries."

Violence did not die out. In 1772 Rhode Islanders boarded a British revenue cutter off Pawtucket, wounded the chief officer, and then burned the ship. The furious British failed to find the conspirators. Committees of Correspondence started by Sam Adams spread to other colonies to coordinate action when needed. Learning of the moves toward civil disobedience, Franklin wrote that "if the oppression continues, a congress may grow out of that correspondence." He pleaded for peaceful protest, fearing that more violence would give Britain the excuse for enlarging the military and putting the colonies under tighter control.

But he himself didn't remain passive. He angered the government by publishing anonymous satires savagely ridiculing its policy and making it appear that it couldn't have done more harm if it had been carefully planned that way. He wrote hoaxes so brilliant that even the shrewdest were taken in by them for a time.

One thing he did created almost a firestorm in England. Thomas Hutchinson, a native of New England, when lieutenant governor of Massachusetts in 1767–1769, had written letters to London urging that the turbulent colonials be restrained by force and their liberties curtailed. An unidentified member of Parliament showed the letters to Franklin in 1772, and with his source's permission, Franklin sent them to Boston for the private information of colonial leaders. Although he insisted the letters not be made public, they were. When London learned of it, a man was wrongly accused of stealing the letters and sending them to Boston.

To exonerate him, Franklin announced that he was the one to send the letters to Boston.

Though it is now clear that the letters were not vital—everyone knew these things anyhow—Franklin found himself the center of a political whirlwind. He was called a thief and a traitor and vilified up and down England as the ringleader of the rebellion. Massachusetts petitioned the Crown to remove Hutchinson from office—he was now the governor—and the Privy Council took it up in January 1774. It would simply have pigeonholed the petition if it had not seen it as a way of attacking Franklin. Franklin got a postponement of the hearings, and while he was preparing his support for the petition, news of the Boston Tea Party reached London. Three ships had anchored in Boston harbor, but the colonials demanded they go back to England without payment of any duty. When Hutchinson refused to permit it, a group of men disguised as Mohawk Indians boarded the ships and threw the cargoes of tea into the harbor.

The Tea Party did not improve London's temper. Its rage with the colonies centered on Franklin. The Americans, it was charged, were mounting a grand conspiracy, and this villain was pulling the strings from London. Forget about the case of Massachusetts versus Hutchinson; this was now the Crown against Franklin. Alexander Wedderburn, the solicitor general, dominated the hearing with an hour-long assault upon Franklin, this "true incendiary," this "secret spring" of revolution, this know-it-all who dared to act like the minister of "a foreign independent state." Franklin was the enemy, the voice of a cause London now saw as perverse and unyielding. No doubt his satires, widely read in England, sharpened the invective.

The members of the Privy Council, making no pretense of considering the petition before them, frequently broke into applause, laughing outright. No one spoke up to say this was not the way to treat the person who was there only to present his colony's petition. If he had done wrong in his handling of the Hutchinson letters, this was not the court for trying that charge.

Through the long, violent personal attack, Franklin stood calm and silent, and when it was over, he went out without a word. His serene manner was never forgotten by the spectators. But he had been defeated, and it stung him badly. He had worked ardently to prevent the breach; nothing he could do now would heal it. If Britain treated petitioners so badly, how could grievances ever be remedied? "Where complaining is a crime," he said, "hope becomes despair."

The petition was thrown out, and the next day Franklin was dismissed from his office of deputy postmaster general in America. It was not only his personal punishment but also a warning to all colonial office-holders to toe the Crown's line or be fired. A few days later he wrote son William that he might be punished for his father's sins and lose his post as governor of New Jersey. "Let them take

*Franklin stands silent before
the lords in Privy Council.*

your place if they want it," he said. It hasn't supported you anyhow. But don't quit, he advised, for "one may make something of an injury, nothing of a resignation."

But all the abuse Britain heaped upon Franklin only restored his old popularity at home. "As a result of this humiliation," wrote Dr. Benjamin Rush, "Franklin is a very popular character in every part of America. He will be received and carried in triumph to his house when he arrives amongst us. It is to be hoped that he will not consent to hold any more [British] offices under government. No step but this can prevent his being handed down to posterity among the first and greatest characters in the world."

In March, Britain decided to punish Boston in a way it would remember. It closed the port of Boston, destroying its commerce, until the town would pay in full for the destroyed tea, and put Massachusetts under the control of the British army commander.

Franklin could do little about it. He knew his usefulness as colonial agent had ended. Who would receive him at court? What Tory leader would listen to him? He could talk only to the opposition, who remained friendly, but were of little help now. He might be arrested too, for the government was seeking evidence to prosecute him for treason.

As he prepared to return home, he learned the colonies planned to meet to decide what to do next. We might have work for you, they wrote. He decided to stay awhile in London. Things were quite bad, but he couldn't believe war—that utter folly—was inevitable. If the Americans kept boycotting British goods, maybe the British merchants and manufacturers would raise such a howl that another ministry would come into power and ensure colonial rights.

Meanwhile, in America the colonies rallied to Boston's support. On Virginia's proposal they met in September 1774 at Philadelphia. The fifty-six delegates decided to retaliate against Britain by cutting off all trade with her. In a Declaration of Rights they told Britain they would not abide by Parliament's laws or the king's word when it infringed upon their liberties. This—the First Continental Congress—demanded repeal of all the offensive acts passed by Parliament since 1763. To follow up, they would meet in a Second Congress in the spring of 1775.

It was not yet revolution, but close to it. The colonies were not demanding to be independent, only to be free to determine their own affairs. No longer would they be treated as children by the mother country. They stood on their own feet and would shape their own future.

Then, on December 19, 1774, Deborah Franklin died, "without a sound." Franklin got the news from William two months later. She had sensed she was going, for she said that if her husband did not return that winter, she doubted she would ever see him again.

In London, Franklin's hope for a new ministry failed. Before the American boycott could do much damage, a quick election returned the Tories to office. Nowhere now was there effective opposition to the harsh policy expressed in the Boston Port Bill. Either the Crown would win, or the colonies. There was no middle way. Franklin, the moderate who had worked for compromise and peace, had come to his great turning point. His dream of reconciliation was shattered. He said that this government which claimed "sovereignty over three millions of virtuous, sensible people in America . . . appeared to have scarce discretion enough to govern a herd of swine."

Stupid, irrational, corrupt men were in power. What room was there for reason? He felt himself become an alien in London. He was "too much of an American" to stay any longer.

In March 1775, he sailed for Philadelphia.

CHAPTER FIFTEEN

WAR TO THE END

Franklin shut himself up in the cabin of the small ship and began writing a long account of what he had been doing in London to prevent war with the colonies. He was sixty-nine now and wanted to get down on paper the record as he understood it. As the packet sailed over calm seas, his pen covered some 250 sheets of paper to create a masterpiece of diplomatic literature.

The pleasant six-week voyage ended on May 5. With Franklin's wife Deborah gone, his daughter, Mrs. Sarah Bache, was now head of the new house built during his absence, and this is where he went to live. He arrived home to find all the colonies united in resistance to Britain. On April 19, just two weeks before his ship anchored at Philadelphia, blood had been spilled in Massachusetts. The king's troops and the colonials had clashed at Lexington and Concord. The British had struck the blow everyone expected, and the Americans had proved they would resist.

But not all of them, by any means. Franklin found his son William standing as a Loyalist on the side of the Crown. We both owe much to Britain, William argued, and have an obligation to her. But Franklin wrote back coldly: You will choose to remain loyal to your master, he said, "but I think independence more honorable than any service." It ended their correspondence for many years.

As couriers rushed the news of Lexington and Concord to all corners of the colonies, delegates to the Second Continental Congress assembled in Philadelphia. Ben had not been home a day before Pennsylvania asked him to represent the colony in the Congress. On May 10 the sessions began. Franklin believed "there never was a good war or a bad peace"; he hoped he could stop the war. But in vain. He saw Philadelphia's volunteers drilling in the fields at five in the morning and again at six in the evening, forming into battalions of infantry, artillery, and cavalry. The Congress met at nine and sat till four. Franklin was put on the Committee of Safety, which met for three hours nightly to plan the defense. In June the Congress chose George Washington chief of the Continental forces, and he hurried to Boston where the American militia surrounded the city held by the Redcoats. Before he arrived, the British captured Breed's Hill (miscalled Bunker Hill) but in a battle that cost them ten times the casualties suffered by the Americans.

Ben wrote to his English friend Bishop Shipley

that the British needlessly and "barbarously" plundered and burned the four hundred houses in undefended Charlestown, killing many civilians. If the Crown expected this savagery to reconcile the Americans, they were mad. Such suffering and loss, even if it went on for twenty years, would not make the Americans submit. He protested when Dr. Samuel Johnson suggested that the slaves be incited to cut their masters' throats and Indians to murder the whites in the back settlements. "This is making war like nations who never had been friends," he said, "and never wish to be such while the world stands." If these things can make a cool old man like me so angry, he wrote, you can imagine what it has done to the general temper here, "which is now little short of madness."

It was a tough task the Congress faced. The sixty-five delegates had to find some way to organize the colonies into a national power. They had to fortify fifteen hundred miles of country; they had to recruit an army and create a navy; they had to arm, train, feed, and house troops, to regulate commerce, negotiate with Indians, seek help abroad. And all without the authority to command action. They could only request, advise, recommend.

Early in July 1775, the Congress issued a "Declaration of the Causes and Necessities of Taking Up Arms." It did not demand independence, it called only for a show of force to bring the Crown to terms. But in London this was taken differently:

the king proclaimed the colonies were in rebellion. It would be a war to the end.

It was now that Franklin wrote his famous letter to his old friend, William Strahan. As a Tory in Parliament, Strahan had voted for those measures that led to Lexington and Concord. In a curious mixture of humor and bitterness, Ben drafted this letter which, though never sent, was often reprinted:

> Mr. Strahan: You are a member of Parliament, and one of that majority which has doomed my country to destruction. You have begun to burn our towns and murder our people. Look upon your hands! They are stained with the blood of your relations! You and I were long friends. You are now my enemy, and I am
>
> > Yours,
> > B. Franklin

Franklin knew it would be a long war. His vastly varied skills were put to work at once. He joined committees to arrange for munitions, to find medical supplies, to select officers, to protect the ports from enemy warships. America would need its own postal service now, and he made Philadelphia the center of a new system, with himself as postmaster general.

As though not busy enough, Franklin was elected to the Pennsylvania legislature and made chairman of the committee to plan defense for the province. He spent three hours early each morning on the colony's affairs, then went off to the Congress at nine. There he worried about how to get gunpowder for Washington's army. It had always come from Europe, and the colonies had no experience manufacturing it. What about using bows and arrows, Ben asked. Not so foolish as it sounds, for back then the muskets were nearly harmless at three hundred yards, and in the time it took to load and fire a bullet a man could shoot four devastating arrows. It would be easier to make bows and arrows than muskets and ammunition.

But what he thought most important to do in the crisis was to plan how this nation struggling to be born would be governed. He revived his old Albany Plan of Union (1754) and read to the Congress his proposal for "Articles of Confederation and Perpetual Union." In considerably modified and diluted form, the Articles of Confederation were adopted in 1777 and sent to the states for their approval. Although not ratified until 1781, it was the first true step toward national union.

In October 1775, Ben was one of a committee of three sent to Cambridge to discuss with Washington ways to supply the army. The general's forces were volunteers soon free to go home; he wanted a new army of twenty thousand men enlisted for a year, and better organized and provisioned. For four days they conferred, giving Washington hope that the colonies would strengthen their support and that Congress would take greater general responsibility for carrying on the war.

His next mission was to try to persuade the Canadians to join the American cause. Earlier an expedition to Canada under Colonel Benedict Arnold had tried to seize Quebec and win over the Canadian provinces. When the expedition failed, Franklin and two other men were sent north to try diplomacy. The party left in April 1776. Snow and ice gripped the land, and twenty-seven harsh days of travel badly weakened the seventy-year-old Franklin. There were only a few hundred British Protestants in Canada, half of them Loyalists. The eighty thousand French Canadians knew how prejudiced the Americans were against Catholics and were not about to give up their religious freedom for union with the colonies below. So the mission failed, and Ben returned to Philadelphia.

He then took up his responsibility as member of a committee dealing with foreign affairs. Its job was to correspond with friends abroad and find out how the European powers might react to requests for help. Its operations were cloaked in such great secrecy that one operator often didn't know what the others were doing. Nor did they trust one another. Under instructions from Franklin, an agent was sent to France to test whether France might enter into a treaty or alliance for commerce or defense, or both. Ben himself wrote to French merchants, offering to barter tobacco for military supplies, and managed to arrange a shipment of arms from the royal arsenal.

It was touchy, dealing with the French. The monarchs of France were absolute rulers of a Catholic country. How would Protestant America look upon a political alliance with it? And would it entangle America in future European wars? Franklin hoped to get military and economic aid without strings, if possible.

As for the French side, they liked the prospect of weakening their old enemy, Britain, and perhaps expanding French influence. It would be useful to have this new America take hold and become friendly to France. But how could a Catholic monarchy help a nation—Protestant at that—make a revolution? And did France have the financial resources to offer aid? In the end, France sent an agent to Philadelphia to inform Franklin's committee that it would be glad to see America independent but could not help much, or openly, until America officially proclaimed itself independent.

That decision was coming closer and closer. In January 1776 Tom Paine published his brilliant pamphlet, *Common Sense*. A poor, unknown Englishman, Paine had become a friend of Franklin's in London. When he emigrated to America in 1774, he carried a letter of introduction from Franklin to his son-in-law Richard Bache of Philadelphia. Paine's appeal for immediate independence quickly sold 150,000 copies, a huge number for that time. His powerful attack on England made clear to Americans that the British system itself, with its monarchy and its inequality, was the enemy. He called not only for independence but also for a representative form of democracy.

He touched a common chord. It was what Americans wanted to hear. Their cry for independence thundered in the ears of Congress. Some of the delegates feared the consequences. Was the time ripe? Would old enemies like France be reliable as allies? On June 7 a Virginia delegate, Richard Henry Lee, introduced a resolution that "these united colonies are, and of right ought to be, free and independent states." Still unsure of itself, the Congress postponed a vote. But it set up a committee—Franklin, Jefferson, Adams, Roger Sherman, and Robert Livingston—to draft a Declaration of Independence—just in case the Congress would agree to one.

It was Jefferson, only thirty-three, who was asked to write the draft, with the helping hands of Franklin and Adams. Franklin offered some small changes, making the language in some places a little less grand, a little more precise, a little stronger. Like many writers, Jefferson suffered when edited. But, as he recalled later, Franklin comforted him by a homely anecdote about a hatter whose handsome new sign began with an elaborate description but was gradually reduced to nothing but the figure of a hat with his name beneath. Simplicity did the job, and did it well.

The committee meets to go over Jefferson's draft of the Declaration of Independence. From left: Franklin, Jefferson, John Adams, Robert Livingston, and Roger Sherman

During many hours of debate, Congress made further changes in the draft, taking out most importantly an attack upon the slave trade. On July 4 the Declaration of Independence was adopted, and then printed. After the delegates signed a parchment copy on August 2, Franklin, according to the legend, said, "Gentlemen, we must now all hang together, or we shall most assuredly hang separately." It was witty, but not a joke. The signers were all, under British law, traitors, and could be executed for what they did.

While serving on the Declaration committee, Ben was chosen chairman of the convention writing a new constitution for Pennsylvania to replace the old colonial charter of William Penn. It meant that at last the old proprietary party was crushed. Franklin put through two of his favorite ideas: that a truly democratic legislature should consist of only one house, and that the executive authority should not be placed in a single person—a governor—but should be exercised by a committee. So the state's executive became a council of twelve members elected by the different counties. It worked so badly that the state constitution was replaced in 1790.

Shortly after the Declaration was signed, a British fleet of two hundred ships with thirty thousand troops landed at what is now Brooklyn. In late August came the Battle of Long Island, when the superior British forces defeated Washington's army. The colonials might have been destroyed if Washington had not staged a masterly retreat. The

*In this picture by Pine and Savage, Franklin is
shown in center foreground, "fast asleep in his chair"
as Congress votes independence.*

British commander proposed an informal peace
conference, and the Congress sent Franklin, John
Adams, and Edmund Rutledge to meet with Lord
Howe on Staten Island. When Howe demanded
that the Declaration of Independence be revoked
before peace negotiations could begin, the conference ended. There was no chance for peace under
such conditions.

A few days later the British occupied New York City as Washington removed his troops to escape being trapped. Congress now appointed a commission of three to negotiate a treaty of alliance with France. Two of the men, Silas Deane and Arthur Lee, were already abroad, and Franklin was named to join them in Paris.

He was over seventy now. The task ahead would be enormously difficult. He was so tired by his multiple duties that he had withdrawn from Pennsylvania's affairs to concentrate his energy on the Congress. "I am old and good for nothing," he said to Dr. Benjamin Rush, but he was still willing to let his country use him for whatever it needed. He loaned the Congress several thousand pounds and deposited his papers for safekeeping with an old friend. For company, he took along his two grandsons, sixteen-year-old Temple, William's son, and Sally's boy, Benjamin Franklin Bache, now seven. They sailed on October 26 on the *Reprisal*, a swift but miserably cramped sloop. They had to evade British cruisers eager to hunt down this distinguished envoy to the court of France. As the ship drove full sail through the November gales, Franklin stayed close to his tiny cabin. Though often sick, he managed daily to take the ocean's temperature to check his theory of the Gulf Stream. Nearing France, the *Reprisal* captured two great British merchantmen, loaded with valuable cargo. For young William and Benjy, it must have been a thrilling adventure. For grandpa, it was one of his worst and most dangerous voyages.

CHAPTER SIXTEEN

DIPLOMAT IN FRANCE

Franklin landed in France on December 3, 1776. He was so weak from his sickness at sea that he could hardly stand. It was a 320-mile journey from the port to Paris, a slow trip on land that took seventeen days. But at every stage of the journey he was greeted with such enthusiasm and acclaim that his spirits soared. The French, he wrote home, are "a most amiable people." To the aristocrats, the scientists, the literary figures he met, this American was a symbol of the New World's simplicity and virtue.

Of course, the French knew Franklin's name well. He had visited their country twice before, in 1767 and 1769. Many of his works had been translated into their language and distributed widely. He was the great scientist, the genius of electricity, the author of *Poor Richard*, the spokesman for the rights of the colonies, an honored associate of their own Academy of Sciences. A two-volume edition of his collected works had been

published in Paris. Beneath the frontispiece portrait
of Franklin were these lines that read, translated
into English:

To steal from Heaven its sacred fire he taught;
The arts to thrive in savage climes he brought;
In the New World the first of Men esteem'd;
Among the Greeks a God he has been deem'd.

This hero worship never let up during the nine
years of his stay in France. It was odd that in this
most absolute of monarchies, this least democratic
of governments, Franklin, the personification of
liberty, should be adored. Of course, a selfish
interest lay underneath: the French detested their
rival empire Great Britain, and nothing would
make the French happier than to see the American
Revolution succeed.

France at this time was ruled by Louis XVI. At
the age of twenty, he had come to the French
throne just two years before Franklin's arrival. His
queen was Marie Antoinette, whom he had married
when he was sixteen and she fifteen. This was
France a dozen years before its own revolution of
1789, a revolution few dreamed of yet. Paris, with
650,000 people, was a city of narrow, cobbled
streets, with the Seine flowing through it, crossed
by bridges lined with shops. The city was sprinkled
with churches and monasteries, dominated by the
cathedral of Notre Dame rising above the Ile de la
Cité on the river. On the wharves along the Seine,

goods and passengers were always loading and unloading. There were public parks and promenades, formal gardens, long boulevards, theaters, and markets. In the Latin Quarter on the left bank lived students and artists, and on the right bank were the homes of the wealthy merchants. Fine highways radiated out from the city to the provinces, built by the monarchy primarily for military use.

It was a country where everything was for the rich, and nothing for the poor. The rich were relatively few, perhaps four thousand aristocrats. Their great privileges included freedom from taxation. They owned the great estates, their sons bishoped the church and officered the army and navy. The peasants bore the burden of taxation and of tithes to the church. The industrial revolution had scarcely touched France yet; it had gone much farther in Britain.

Yet there was the beginning of a public awakening in France. The first daily newspaper appeared just after Franklin arrived, and soon there were dozens of periodicals. What the writers of the Enlightenment had to say about freedom, reason, and humanitarianism was circulated in translations and through pamphlets that educated people of all classes. France had her own stars of the Enlightenment—the philosophers Voltaire and Montesquieu and Rousseau, the encyclopedist Diderot, the economist Turgot, and the naturalist Buffon. Franklin knew their works and met some of these thinkers, and they were familiar with his accomplishments.

Popular as he was, the French government could not formally receive Franklin as diplomat. It wasn't sure whether the revolution would succeed, and awaited some guarantee of victory before recognizing the American government.

Franklin lived for a time in hotels, then early in 1777 moved to Passy. It was a lovely village just beyond Paris, lying on a hill beside the Seine. (Today it is part of Paris itself.) Handsome villas and royal chateaus dominated the village, with a parish church, a small theater, and houses and shops clustered around them.

His landlord at Passy was Jacques-Donatien Le Ray deChaumont, a wealthy shipping magnate, slave trader, and army supplier. His was a spacious estate, with terraces, gardens, groves of linden trees, and a lake. Paris was only two miles off and the royal palace at Versailles ten miles away. Chaumont befriended Franklin because he hoped to profit by the sale of munitions to the Americans. Franklin, of course, delighted in the small wing of the luxurious house rented to him, and he expected to make use of Chaumont's power and influence. Chaumont proved generous to the American cause, for later he would spend almost his entire fortune of two million francs on it and eventually go bankrupt.

While posing as a simple and modest man before the French public, Franklin lived like an aristocrat

*Walking the streets of Paris, Franklin
is the center of attention.*

at Passy. He kept nine servants, a coachman with carriage and horses, a cellar of over a thousand bottles of wine, and plenty of his favorite rum. He ate royally too, as the accounts he kept show. This was lavish living, said some critical Americans who witnessed it. Franklin replied that frugality was "a virtue I never could acquire in myself." Besides, didn't he save quite a bit by dining out as a guest six days in seven? And hadn't he always said the hope of good living was the spur to hard work and enterprise?

Franklin kept Temple with him but sent Benjy to Geneva, to attend a good school "where he will be educated a Republican and a Protestant, which could not be so conveniently done at the schools in France."

He entertained often at Passy, usually on Sundays, nursing friendships among those French who could advance his goal of an alliance with their government. He found many influential supporters. Everyone enjoyed his company, for he knew how to direct the talk at table. "One of the rules which made Dr. Franklin the most amiable of men in society," said Thomas Jefferson, was "never to contradict anybody. If he was urged to announce an opinion, he did it either by asking questions, as if for information, or by suggesting doubts."

Franklin himself laid down the rule he followed:

The wit of conversation consists more in finding it in others, than showing a great deal yourself. He who goes out of your company pleased with his own facetiousness and ingenuity will the sooner come into it again. Most men had rather please than admire you, and seek less to be instructed and diverted, than approved and applauded, and it is certainly the most delicate sort of pleasure, to please another.

Franklin was very much aware of the impression he made upon others. Early on, as we've seen, he developed a sense of self that he projected upon the public. By the time he arrived as ambassador to France, his face was displayed all over Europe— in busts, statues, paintings, engravings. In Paris he sat for many portraits by the leading artists, "so often," he said, "that I am perfectly sick of it. I know of nothing so tedious as sitting hours in one fixed posture." Still, he kept doing it. It helped the cause and pleased his ego.

His portrait decorated medallions and snuff-boxes, rings and watches, bracelets and looking glasses, and even a chamber pot Louis XVI gave to a countess. "My face is as well known as that of the moon," he wrote his daughter. "Incredible numbers" of my pictures are sold, he added.

This was the beginning of the modern means of creating celebrity by the visual image. The engraving and printing trade was expanding in a rush; much of its product was the reproduction of portraits of famous people, thus making them still

*The cover of a snuffbox pictures the wise
old American with France's esteemed
philosophers, Voltaire (left) and Rousseau.*

more famous. The rich could buy statues and
paintings, but for all the others there were cheap
engravings, plates, pitchers featuring the faces of
the illustrious. What's especially noteworthy about
Franklin was that he didn't look like the traditional
"great man," but rather like Everyman, any ordi-
nary mortal. This was a new kind of hero, emerging
from a revolutionary era. He was the man who

came up out of nowhere to represent the human potential in all of us.

Franklin understood the propaganda value of his image. He played up to it by the way he costumed himself and staged his appearances. Over his unpowdered gray hair he wore an old fur hat that came down his forehead about to his spectacles. He dressed very plainly, and his manner in company was open and direct, in deliberate contrast to the elegant fashions and exquisite manners of the aristocrats who surrounded him.

"Few strangers in France have had the good fortune to be so universally popular," he wrote his sister. He was taken up by powerful members of the court who openly endorsed the cause of the rebels. But conservative nobles didn't think it so wise to support a revolution against a monarchy. Others believed the Americans would win in the long run but needed no help to do it. And still others were against giving aid to the Americans because it would cost France too much. Franklin wrote a friend that most Europeans wanted liberty for themselves but despaired of winning it from their rulers. They read translations of the democratic constitutions of the various colonies "with rapture," and they talked eagerly of emigrating to America as soon as peace and independence would be established. It is "a common observation here, that our cause is the cause of all mankind, and that we are fighting for their liberty in defending our own."

The French foreign minister, Charles Gravier Vergennes, believed in "divide and rule" and was ready to use any means to weaken Britain. So was Spain, but neither country was ready to enter an open alliance with the rebels. Still, they were eager to use America as a weapon against their common enemy, Britain. France set up a secretly subsidized dummy company to send munitions, tents, and clothing for Washington's troops, and Spain provided similar help. When the French ships arrived in America, they carried the first military volunteers too, and soon Lafayette followed with many other soldiers. A key figure in these clandestine operations was Beaumarchais, courtier, dramatist, inventor, adventurer, who, like many other Frenchmen, lost most of his money helping the Americans.

What Franklin kept pressing on Vergennes was a treaty of commerce and friendship, together with a request for manned ships, muskets, and ammunition. While the French would not yet accept that, they continued to provide secret help through large offers of credit. The treaty prospect was dim so long as Washington could report little military success. Meanwhile, Franklin's agents in other parts of Europe bargained for military aid with offers of American tobacco, rice, sugar, and indigo.

As he dickered for help wherever he could, Franklin was battered by requests from Congress for more and more military material and the loans to pay for it. He pushed the French to the point where their neutrality became almost a joke. France loaned America millions of dollars, let volunteers enlist, permitted American warships to use its harbors. The volunteers were another burden for Franklin. Hundreds of French and other Europeans wanted to gain commissions as officers in the American army. It took great care to weed out the unsuitable from the applicants who promised to be really valuable.

As he had done earlier during his mission to Britain, he used the press brilliantly to advance his aims. He wrote many articles for both French and European publications, salting them with wit and satire, and followed closely what others wrote to see how he might intervene to shape public opinion. He carried on a broad correspondence with friends both old and new, rallying support for the Americans. His relations with the other American commissioners in Europe were not very good. There was envy, rivalry, and mistrust on all sides, sometimes warranted, sometimes not, and even charges of corruption, inevitable when large sums of money are involved. The infighting went on for almost two years, until Franklin became the sole American diplomat in Paris.

Spies were everywhere. One American, Edward Bancroft, turned out to be an agent on the British payroll. While he served Franklin and the other commissioners as secretary for some seven years, his spying for the British helped to capture many munitions ships headed for the United States. Not until a hundred years later was Bancroft's treachery discovered. Expecting espionage, Franklin's rule, he said, was "to be concerned in no affairs that I should blush to have made public, and to do nothing but what spies may see and welcome."

Through it all, Franklin's energy, humor, patience, tact, his understanding of people and politics, served the United States superbly. Few others could have done so well. But despite his genius, little would have come of his mission if events had not made a great change. In October 1777 General Burgoyne lost a major battle to the Americans at Saratoga. He was forced to surrender his entire army: a glorious victory for the Americans and a disaster for the British.

It was early in December before the great news reached Franklin at Passy. Swiftly Franklin completed negotiations for an alliance with the French. Saratoga convinced the European enemies of Britain that this was the time to settle old scores. No longer was there any doubt how the war would end. On February 5, 1778, the documents were signed. For the ceremony, Franklin dressed in the suit of velvet he had worn the day Wedderburn had attacked him so viciously before the Privy Council in London. He never wore it again.

Two treaties were signed: one of amity and commerce, the other an alliance for mutual defense. "The great principle in both treaties," Franklin wrote, "is a perfect equality and reciprocity; no advantage being demanded by France, or privileges of commerce, which the States may not grant to any and every other nation. . . . The King has treated us generously and magnanimously, taking no advantage of our present difficulties to exact terms which we would not willingly grant when established in prosperity and power."

France, now the open ally of the Americans, prepared to send a fleet and an army to fight alongside General Washington. Spain would soon join France in sending aid, and then Holland. It was the fruit of the most important success of Franklin's diplomatic career. In March, Louis XVI officially received Franklin in the Palace of Versailles and soon named a minister to the United States. The Congress ratified the treaties in May, and in September elected Franklin to the post of minister to France.

CHAPTER SEVENTEEN

"I LOVE THE LADIES"

His success as a diplomat Franklin matched with his success in the salons. To the ladies of Paris he was "mon cher Papa." Even while raising arms and funds for his country, he found time to court the ladies. French society permitted the paying of frank compliments, and Franklin's wit found full play in conversation and correspondence. To a Boston step-niece he wrote, "Somebody, it seems, gave it out that I loved ladies; and then everybody presented me their ladies (or the ladies presented themselves) to be embraced— that is, to have their necks kissed. For as to kissing of lips or cheeks, it is not the mode here, the first is reckoned rude, and the other may rub off the paint. The French ladies have, however, 1,000 other ways of rendering themselves agreeable."

There are stories of half a dozen women with whom he had affectionate relationships during his years in France. One of the younger was Anne-Louise Brillon de Jouy. Thirty-six when she met him, she was a beautiful and intelligent woman married to a man twenty years her senior. He was a government official who acted as intermediary for French merchants selling weapons to the Americans. Franklin, of course, was almost forty years older than Madame Brillon, but she found age no barrier to the enjoyment of his company. An excellent musician, she and her daughters entertained Franklin "with little concerts, a cup of tea and a game of chess," often seeing him twice a week at her home in Passy. He wrote his famous Bagatelles for her and other intimate friends, printing them on his private press in his house at Passy. These are short essays, charming and whimsical.

Once, addressing Madame Brillon as "my very dear daughter," and referring to a siege of gout, he said, "When I was a young man and enjoyed more of the favors of the sex than I do at present, I had no gout at all. So, if the ladies of Passy had more of that kind of Christian charity which I have so often vainly recommended to you, I should not be having the gout now. This seems to me good logic."

A still more intimate friend was Madame Helvetius, a wealthy widow in her sixties who lived at Auteuil. She was noted for her beauty in youth and was still very attractive. She held a weekly salon that drew people like Franklin and Voltaire. She and Franklin hugged and kissed each other in public, a display that "highly disgusted" Abigail Adams, who said she didn't want to know "ladies of this cast." Franklin asked—we don't know how seriously—to marry Madame Helvetius, a proposal she declined amiably, without losing his friendship.

As confidence in the ultimate victory of his cause rose, Franklin showed himself more and more in public—this despite the poor health he suffered in his seventies. To a doctor, he wrote that he was "subject to slight fits of the gout at long intervals; was accustomed to what is called good living, used but little exercise, being from the nature of his employment as well as from love of books, much in his chamber writing or reading."

For a few years running he made systematic notes on his health, maintaining a cool curiosity about his symptoms and their possible causes. He mentions gout, of course, and fever, boils, scabs, dropsy, itching, scurf, giddiness, loosening teeth, always indicating what remedies he tried and whether or not they helped. At one point he remarked that "I have as much vigor and activity as can be expected at my age."

He remained skeptical about highly touted new cures. "There being so many disorders which cure themselves," he wrote, "and such a disposition in mankind to deceive themselves and one another on these occasions, and living long has given me so frequent opportunity of seeing certain remedies cried up as curing everything, and yet soon after laid aside as totally useless," that he had come to expect most such claims would prove a delusion.

He never lost the keen edge of his interest in

science. The speed of its progress, he wrote Joseph Priestley, made him regret that he was born too soon. Who could imagine the heights to which man's power over nature might be carried in the next centuries? His letter anticipates man's ability to fly through space, to ease the labor of agriculture, to prevent or cure disease, to lengthen the span of life. And then he adds sorrowfully: "O that moral science were in as fair a way of improvement, that men would cease to be wolves to one another, and that human beings would at length learn what they now improperly call humanity!"

He was fascinated by French experiments with balloons and watched the first time passengers went aloft in one. When two men crossed the English channel in a balloon, they brought this veteran postmaster general the first piece of airmail. He predicted that five thousand balloons carrying troops into surprise raids on enemy territory might make combat so terrible that it would convince sovereigns of the folly of warfare. He sent a French philologist his observations on the languages of American Indians and published a pamphlet that illustrated how superior were the Indians' rules of common civility manifested in their public councils, as compared with the rudeness in the British House of Commons.

A letter of Franklin's on the cruel criminal laws of the time blames them on the desire of the rich to protect their property. People are hanged for stealing a strip of cloth worth a few shillings, he says, and asks, "Is there no difference in value between property and life?" He attacks too the unjust wars nations wage against their neighbors: "Justice is as strictly due between neighbor nations as between neighbor citizens. A highwayman is as much a robber when he plunders in a gang as when single; and a nation that makes an unjust war is only a great gang."

Prosperous and prominent as he himself was, he did not forget the working class he sprang from. At Passy he wrote "Reflections on Wages," which attributes the rise in technology "in a great degree to the workmen. There is no important manufacture in which they have not invented some useful process which saves time and materials or improves the workmanship." Yet the wages of the people "who live solely by the labor of their hands . . . secures so scanty a subsistence that, barely able to provide for their own necessities, they have not the means of marrying and rearing a family, and are reduced to beggary whenever employment fails them, or age and sickness oblige them to give up work."

Yet, he went on, many hard hearts believe that people must be poor to keep them down, while they claim that it is in the interests of business to keep wages low so that prices not go too high. He called these views cruel and unfeeling, and after countering such arguments, reminded governments not to forget that "the object of every political society ought to be the happiness of the largest number."

Received as the American ambassador at the
royal palace of Versailles, Franklin is
crowned with a laurel wreath as Louis XVI and
Marie Antoinette, seated at right, watch.

Now that Franklin was officially the ambassador
from America, he moved more freely in public. He
appeared at the opera and theater, where crowds
applauded him, and gave a party to celebrate the
thirteen United States. At a meeting of the Royal
Academy of Sciences it was noticed that both Franklin and Voltaire, who had never met, were present.
The audience insisted the two great men should
greet one another and would not desist until they
embraced and kissed on both cheeks, French style.

Meanwhile, the long, drawn-out war in America moved toward its end. It was the support of the French that made a huge difference. In July 1780 they sent over General Rochambeau with five thousand troops, and in 1781 a powerful naval force arrived commanded by Admiral de Grasse. Despite its own shaky economy, France made the Americans still more loans for arms, equipment, food, and back pay owed the troops.

General Washington planned a strategy with the French that would bring their forces together in the Chesapeake Bay region. Meanwhile, the British general Lord Cornwallis moved up to Virginia and camped on the York River at Yorktown. The French fleet blocked the sea entrance to Yorktown, thus keeping Sir Henry Clinton's fleet from sailing down from New York to rescue Cornwallis. And American and French troops blocked the land entrance to the York peninsula, barring that escape route for Cornwallis. As his food and supplies dwindled and the guns of France and America pounded his forces, Cornwallis saw no way out. On October 19, 1781, he surrendered his entire army of seven thousand men.

Washington sent an express rider galloping north to Philadelphia to bring the glorious news to Congress. A frenzied celebration exploded. It took a month for the news to reach London and Paris. Sporadic fighting went on for another year, but when the French defeated the British in the West Indies, Britain realized it was all over for her. The

House of Commons voted to end the war and make peace with the Americans.

Franklin, together with John Jay and John Adams, formed the commission to negotiate the peace. The three men met daily in Paris in an atmosphere of mutual suspicion because of differing personalities as well as views on how to deal with Britain and France. But by November 1782 they and the British negotiators could agree on a preliminary draft of the peace treaty. With Britain making liberal concessions, the Americans won the basic points Franklin insisted upon. The final treaty was signed at Versailles on September 3, 1783. Its former colonies, Britain agreed, were now "free, sovereign and independent." France approved the outcome, especially because it was at the expense of its old foe. But the war had cost her so enormously that it would contribute to bringing on the French Revolution in 1789.

With the war over and the treaty concluded, Franklin asked Congress to recall him. But it was in no hurry to release him. He went on handling America's commercial affairs and treaties with the few other European powers ready to recognize the new nation. To give all Europeans a true picture of his democratic republic, he published the texts of the Articles of Confederation and all the state constitutions.

He kept up a correspondence with his old British friends, the intellectuals who spoke for a new age of freedom that America had now ushered

*The American Commission meets to discuss
preliminary peace negotiations with
Great Britain. John Jay, John Adams, Franklin,
Henry Laurens and Temple Franklin are shown
by the painter, Benjamin West. The blank space
was left for the two British commissioners,
but they failed to sit for the artist.*

in. Yet he never anticipated the revolution that would soon erupt in France. He knew well how bitterly exploited were the peasants and workers of France, but he still saw Louis XVI as a benevolent ruler in no danger of being overthrown. In this he failed an ambassador's duty to observe and report back home the true facts.

Almost seventy-eight, Franklin was losing so many friends to death that he felt there was little reason to go on living. When he heard that Margaret Stevenson, his old London landlady and friend, had died, he wrote her daughter Polly of his grief, then added:

> At length we are in peace, God be praised, and long, very long, may it continue! All wars are follies, very expensive, and very mischievous ones. When will mankind be convinced of this, and agree to settle their difference by arbitration? Were they to do it, even by the cast of a die, it would be better than by fighting and destroying each other.

And then he added: "The fewer we become, the more let us love one another."

Not until May 1785 did the Congress allow Franklin to leave his post. In July, at the age of seventy-nine, too feeble to walk or ride, he was taken out of Passy on one of the king's litters carried by mules. Along his journey to the port, flowers were tossed in his path, and crowds halted the procession to honor him. He crossed the Channel to Southampton for a chilly meeting with his son William and saw the Shipley family for the last time.

His packet reached Philadelphia on September 14. As Franklin was carried down the Market Street wharf, guns fired and church bells rang to welcome him home.

CHAPTER EIGHTEEN

"THIS IS MY COUNTRY"

No sooner had Franklin landed in Philadelphia than he was made president of Pennsylvania's Supreme Council, a position something like today's governor. He came home intending to avoid public duties, but he couldn't resist the call for his counsel. My country's folk, he joked, have taken "the prime of my life. They have eaten my flesh and seem resolved to pick my bones."

Franklin moved into the house he had built behind Market Street, but it no longer held the family as it once was. Deborah was ten years gone, and his son William was in exile in England. Now he would live with his daughter Sally Bache and three of her children. He soon found the house too cramped for comfort and set about adding two bedrooms and a big library for his scientific instruments and the eighteen large boxes of books he had brought from France. "I hardly know how to justify building a library at an age that will so soon oblige me to quit it," he wrote his sister Jane, "but we are apt to forget that we are grown old, and building is an amusement."

In these last years of life, when illness confined him so often to bed, his library, with over four thousand volumes, was his chief pleasure. It was probably the best private library in America, and he delighted in showing its treasures to visitors. When pain was not too crippling, he amused himself with reading and writing, and in conversation with friends. One of his granddaughters recalled that when she was little, he had her bring her Webster spelling book and say her lessons to him. Under his direction, his grandson, Benjamin Franklin Bache, the printer, published some books for children. Franklin tried them with little boys and girls and found that the fun they got from them speeded up their progress in reading.

The house had a small garden and a lawn with a large mulberry tree. He often sat under the tree while chatting with visitors on summer afternoons. On winter evenings he passed the time playing cards. He wrote his old friend, Bishop Shipley, that a man with a large family "is a broader mark for sorrow, but stands a broader mark for pleasure too." As for himself, he had "many reasons to like living. But the course of nature must soon put a period to my present mode of existence. This I shall submit to with less regret, as having seen during a long life a good deal of this world, I feel a growing curiosity to be acquainted with some other. . . ."

At home in Philadelphia, Franklin and his family entertain visitors at tea in the garden.

In the spring of 1786, gout and kidney stones
made it impossible for Franklin to ride on horse-
back or in a carriage. If only the new balloons he
had seen aloft in France were as common as
carriages to get him around painlessly! Meanwhile,
he began to move about town in a sedan chair,
carried by convicts trusted to his service. Wryly he
said he hoped that in some future state, he would
"not only be as well as I was, but a little better."
For he believed that he would, in some shape or
other, always exist. When nature wasted not even
a drop of water, how could souls be annihilated?
Could God "suffer the daily waste of millions of
minds ready made that now exist, and put himself
to the continual trouble of making new ones?"

Always keeping his eye on politics, he saw that
the new government of the United States was
working badly under the Articles of Confederation.
Each of the thirteen states was acting like a sovereign, independent unit. They associated with one
another only loosely in the Confederation. They
quarreled among themselves over boundary lines,
tariffs, court decisions. Their differences were
sharpened by the hard times that had followed the
Revolutionary War.

To keep the Union from falling apart, many
people began to call for a strong central authority.
The states agreed that a national convention should
meet in Philadelphia in May 1787. Its aim would
be to strengthen the existing government so that it
could better meet the needs of all. Fifty-five dele-

gates from twelve of the thirteen states (Rhode Island stayed home) showed up at the Pennsylvania State House (later called Independence Hall). Over half the men were under forty, but they brought rich experience in the world's ways. Among them were planters and businessmen, soldiers and merchants, governors and legislators, inventors and lawyers, and one professional writer—Benjamin Franklin. At eighty-two, he was by far the oldest delegate, and one of the eight chosen by his state.

While this was home to Franklin, the other delegates were guests at private houses and spent many of their evenings plotting strategy in the town's taverns. In the convention, they worked behind closed doors so they could debate the issues without pressure and then submit their conclusions to the people. But it was hard to keep the talkative Franklin quiet. At the convivial dinners he gave in his home, a "discreet member" of the convention was usually present to head off the conversation whenever the old man seemed about to disclose a secret.

One guest in his home during the convention was Manasseh Cutler, a Massachusetts clergyman, who was eager to meet "the great man who had been the wonder of Europe as well as the glory of America." He was astonished to find Franklin "a short, fat, trunched old man, in a plain Quaker dress, bald pate, and short white locks, sitting without his hat under the tree. . . . His voice was low, but his countenance open, frank and pleasing."

The delegates met off and on for four months that hot summer. No more than thirty were ever present at any one session. After setting some ground rules, they agreed that revising the Articles of Confederation wouldn't do. They threw it aside to take up a Virginia Plan offered by James Madison. Only thirty-six, he was a small shy man with a weak voice. But he had come to Philadelphia having thought out more deeply than others the nation's crucial problem: how to create a central government that would be strong and effective while protecting the interests of the states and ensuring that the central power would not be abused. Setting the terms of debate, his plan provided for the separation of powers among the three main branches of government—legislative, executive, and judicial—and for checks and balances to assure that no branch could seize control and exercise tyranny.

Sick as he was, Franklin never missed a session. Not an orator, he was valued rather for his great prestige and his political skill at compromise. His very presence, together with George Washington's, assured the people that this extraordinary endeavor might succeed. His humor, his conciliatory tone, calmed hot tempers and brought the delegates to listen to the opposition's arguments and seek common grounds.

The principles and forms of the constitution they were shaping at Philadelphia did not spring from nowhere. The framers had absorbed much from historians and philosophers. Their work also grew out of two hundred years of experience with colonial charters and constitutions. Plans for uniting the colonies had been offered before, and Franklin's Albany proposal of 1754 was one of the most important. He had also helped to frame the new constitution for Pennsylvania in 1776. Now, in 1787, he was carrying out the most significant work of his life. He was so weak that he could not remain standing for any length of time on the convention floor. The most important things he had to say he wrote out and had his colleague, James Wilson, read to the delegates. So we have his speeches preserved intact in the notes of the debates kept by Madison.

From so old and feeble a man perhaps little could be expected. And some of the proposals he made, though always received respectfully, were ignored as whimsical or useless. But he suggested other ideas that were strong and valuable. He vigorously opposed any property restrictions for voters or members of Congress. Some of the greatest rogues he had known were the richest, he said. He favored a clause allowing the president to be impeached for high crimes and misdemeanors. (Better this, he said, than the traditional method of assassination.) And he was against allowing the president an absolute veto on legislation. He wanted all money matters to be made public to forestall cries of corruption, and he demanded there be positive proof against anyone charged with treason.

The fifty-five delegates agreed on some broad issues—faith in republican government and the need for checks and balances—but they held widely diverse views on what government should do and how it should do it. At times it seemed the convention was "scarce held together by the strength of a hair," as one delegate put it. Would this experiment in writing a democratic constitution fail? One of the major issues splitting the convention was the division of power between the smaller and larger states. After intense wrangling, Franklin spoke up in the plain words of a craftsman:

> When a broad table is to be made, and the edges of the planks do not fit, the artist takes a little from both, and makes a good joint. In like manner here both sides must part with some of their demands, in order that they may join in some accomodating proposition.

At this critical moment he made one of his major contributions. He helped settle the issue of how much representation should be given to the smaller states, who feared being dominated by the larger ones if representation in both House and Senate were to be in proportion to population. His great compromise united the two factions by proposing that each state have an equal number of delegates in the Senate (two for every state), while in the lower House representation should be in proportion to population. Thus, he satisfied everybody, and his plan became a fundamental principle of the Constitution. Without it, there might have been no federal union.

Another major compromise dealt with slavery. This was the dominant issue between North and South. At least twenty-five of the fifty-five delegates owned slaves; perhaps they felt self-conscious sitting here in Philadelphia, whose prominent abolitionists believed that the slave trade was America's greatest weakness. The abolitionists thought it hypocritical to proclaim that "all men are created free and equal" in a society that tolerated slavery.

This June of 1787 the Pennsylvania Society for Promoting the Abolition of Slavery—whose president was Benjamin Franklin—met and adopted a petition imploring the Constitutional Convention to "make the suppression of the African slave trade in the United States a part of their important deliberations." The secretary, Tench Coxe, handed the petition to Franklin, but with the advice that this was not the right time to seek action. Franklin must have agreed, for he said nothing about it, and the delegates never took it up. A realist, he knew that the convention, nearly half of it slaveholding, would not vote to suppress the slave trade. It was certain to break up if a majority tried to shove indigestible motions down the throats of so large a minority.

Instead, the pro- and antislavery factions reached a compromise. Their first job was to build a nation. So they allowed slavery to remain legal to keep the lower South, where it was important for the production of major crops, in the Union. And they agreed to allow the South to count three-fifths of its slaves as a basis for representation in Congress. The African slave trade would not be interfered with for another twenty years. And the states were required to return fugitive slaves to their masters.

It was recognition of slavery as a fact, not approval of it. But even as the Convention adopted these clauses, the Congress, meeting in New York, enacted the Northwest Ordinance. It prohibited slavery north of the Ohio River, where the slave-owners had hoped to expand their power as new states would come into the Union.

Years later, Madison wrote to Lafayette that the question of emancipation was not raised at the Convention because "any allusion to the subject . . . would have been a spark to a mass of gunpowder."

In September the delegates reached a final draft of the Constitution. Franklin believed the Convention should adopt it unanimously. On Monday, September 17, the day the document was to be signed, he rose and asked the delegates to listen while the speech he had written the day before would be read out for him by James Wilson. It was a calm appeal to reason:

> I confess that I do not entirely approve of this Constitution at present, but, Sir, I am not sure I shall never approve it: For having

lived long, I have experienced many instances of being obliged, by better information or fuller consideration, to change opinions even on important subjects, which I once thought right, but found to be otherwise. It is therefore that the older I grow the more apt I am to doubt my own judgment, and to pay more respect to the judgment of others. Most men, indeed, as well as most sects in religion, think themselves in possession of all truth, and that wherever others differ from them it is so far error. . . . But though many private persons think almost as highly of their own infallibility as of that of their sect, few express it so naturally as a certain French lady who, in a little dispute with her sister, said, I don't know how it happens, sister, but I meet with nobody but myself that's always in the right.

In these sentiments, Sir, I agree to this Constitution, with all its faults, if they are such; because I think a general government necessary for us, and there is no form of government but what may be a blessing to the people if well administered; and I believe further that this is likely to be well administered for a course of years, and can only end in despotism, as other forms have done before it, when the people shall become so corrupted as to need despotic government, being incapable of any other.

I doubt, too, whether any other convention we can obtain may be able to make a better Constitution: for when you assemble a number of men to have the advantage of their joint wisdom, you inevitably assemble with those men all their prejudices, their passions, their errors of opinion, their local interests, and their selfish views. From such an assembly can a perfect production be expected? It therefore astonishes me, Sir, to find this system approaching so near to perfection as it does; and I think it will astonish our enemies, who are waiting with confidence to hear that our councils are confounded, like those of the builders of Babel, and that our states are on the point of separation, only to meet hereafter for the purpose of cutting one another's throats.

Thus I consent, Sir, to this Constitution because I expect no better and because I am not sure that it is not the best. The opinions I have had of its errors I sacrifice to the public good. I have never whispered a syllable of them abroad. Within these walls they were born, and here they shall die. If every one of us in returning to our constituents were to report the objections he has had to it, and use his influence to gain partisans in support of them, we might prevent its being generally received, and thereby lose all the salutary effects and great advantages resulting naturally in our favor among foreign nations, as well as among ourselves, from our real or apparent unanimity.

Much of the strength and efficiency of any government, in procuring and securing happiness to the people depends on opinion, on the general opinion of the goodness of that government as well as of the wisdom and integrity of its governors. I hope, therefore, that for our own sakes, as a part of the people, and for the sake of our posterity, we shall act heartily and unanimously in recommending this Constitution, wherever our influence may extend, and turn our future thoughts and endeavors to the means of having it well administered.

On the whole, Sir, I cannot help expressing a wish that every member of the convention, who may still have objections to it, would with me on this occasion doubt a little of his own infallibility, and to make manifest our unanimity, put his name to this instrument.

His words, reprinted in more than fifty newspapers, would exert the most decisive influence during the heated debates in the states over ratification. Nine of the thirteen states had to approve the Constitution for it to go into effect. With Delaware the first to ratify and New Hampshire the ninth (all thirteen finally came in), the Constitution became the fundamental law of the new nation on March 4, 1789.

Toward the end of 1787 Franklin's kidney affliction became even worse after he took a bruising fall on the stone steps that led to his garden. But in 1788 he resumed sending letters to the press and publishing essays defending freedom of the press and attacking the slave trade. In February 1790 he signed an antislavery memorial to the first Congress, on behalf of the Pennsylvania abolition society. It was his final public act. A few weeks later, less than a month before his death, his last political essay appeared, a letter to the *Federal Gazette* ridiculing a congressman's defense of slavery.

On April 30, 1789, George Washington took the oath of office as president of the newly constituted United States. "Our grand machine has at length begun to work," said Franklin. "I pray God to bless and guide its operations. If any form of government is capable of making a nation happy, ours I think bids fair now for producing that effect. But after all, much depends upon the people who are to be governed. . . ."

Six months later, the first Congress to meet under the new Constitution completed its session. This was the Congress that adopted the Bill of Rights as the first ten amendments to the Constitution. Franklin wrote he was pleased that it had done its work "with a greater degree of temper, prudence and unanimity than could well have been expected, and our future prospects seem very favorable." The French Revolution had just begun—a "truly surprising" explosion, he thought, hoping it would end in establishing a good constitution for that country. But the violent convulsions appalled him. Two of his best French friends had died, one assassinated and the other guillotined.

By this time, after serving three years as president of Pennsylvania, Franklin was ready to give up all public business. His friends came often to visit him, and his eight grandchildren by his daughter Sally played with and amused him. He began Part Three of his long-delayed *Autobiography*, carrying the story only to his fiftieth year. Again he did not rely much on his papers but wrote mostly out of his memory. He sent off copies of the three parts to friends in Europe and then, feeling a bit stronger, added a few more pages. (The whole *Autobiography* was not published until 1868, after the original manuscript was discovered in Paris.)

He spent his last year confined to bed, suffering such constant pain from the kidney stone that he was forced to take opium. It gave him relief but wore him down. He lost his appetite and wasted away to little but a skeleton covered with skin. A few days before the end, a fever seized him, and when he groaned with pain, he apologized for not bearing it as he should. Then calmness came on, and on April 17, 1790, about 11:00 P.M., he died quietly, at exactly eighty-four years and three months.

Epitaph written 1728.

The Body of
B Franklin Printer,
(Like the Cover of an old Book
Its Contents torn out
And stript of its Lettering & Gilding)
Lies here, Food for Worms.
But the Work shall not be lost;
For it will, (as he believ'd) appear once more,
In a new and more elegant Edition
Revised and corrected,
By the Author.

At the age of twenty-two
Franklin wrote this epitaph
for himself, playing on
his occupation as printer.

He was buried in Christ Church Burial Ground. A crowd of twenty thousand people came, the largest Philadelphia had ever seen. On his tomb are the plain words he wanted: BENJAMIN AND DEBORAH FRANKLIN 1790.

In one of his last letters—to David Hartley, a British friend—Franklin wrote:

> God grant that not only the love of liberty, but a thorough knowledge of the rights of man, may pervade all the nations of the earth, so that a philosopher may set his foot anywhere on its surface, and say, "This is my country."

A NOTE ON SOURCES

In writing this biography, I was constantly tempted to let Benjamin Franklin speak in his own voice. No matter what the topic, I found he had something to say about it. And with a wit and pungency few could match. For these quotations I drew from several collections of Franklin's writings. The most exhaustive is the multivolume *The Papers of Benjamin Franklin*. The first volume appeared in 1959, after a global search (it still continues) for every surviving document and letter Franklin wrote and every letter written to him. Published by Yale University Press, the series has been edited first by Leonard W. Labaree, then by William B. Willcox, Claude-Anne Lopez, and now by Barbara B. Oberg. In 1987, volume 25 appeared, taking us into 1778, when Franklin reached the age of seventy-two. He lived another twelve years, which will require another twenty-five volumes to be published over the next few decades. The editors' annotation provides the historical context for the thousands of documents.

The reader might like to know a little about how such a vast collection of papers is put together. I have had some experience of this myself, in collecting and editing the correspondence of Lydia Maria Child, the nineteenth-century writer and advocate of abolition and women's rights. It took our group four years to find and publish some twenty-six hundred letters. Imagine how much more difficult and costly it has been to chase down the Franklin papers. They include not only letters sent and received but also essays, business ledgers, invoices, receipts, even household accounts.

Many of Franklin's letters were destroyed or lost in his lifetime. Large numbers were deposited in various places (including a stable) in America or Europe, and often some were distributed as souvenirs of a great man or were sold to autograph collectors. Franklin's letters went to friends in America and abroad, and dealt with business, political, scientific, and personal affairs. During his long life he wrote to several thousand different people. (All this long before the typewriter or word processor.) Adding to the editors' burden was the search for his printed pamphlets, letters, and essays published in newspapers. Some of these he signed, for others he used a pen name, and still others had to be identified by other means.

Going by my own experience in this field, such a project requires extensive correspondence with all possible sources of the papers you are after, and follow-up visits to many of them—university, state, and municipal libraries, state and local historical societies, and to individuals who may hold only a letter or two but who may also be able to steer you to other sources. No place, say the Franklin people, was too improbable to hold a Franklin letter. An unexpected delight is to find not only something you believed to be there but also other things you had not known about. Editors, the Yale staff says, begin as scholars but become sleuths and venture-some serendipitists as well.

More easily available to the general reader than the Yale edition are many one-volume anthologies of Franklin's words. Almost all of these are centered upon his *Autobiography* (which goes up to the age of fifty) but with considerable excerpts too from Franklin's letters, pamphlets, journalism, *Poor Richard's Almanack*, the Bagatelles, his writings on electricity, and a myriad other aspects of his scientific investigations. The most recent of these collections is *Franklin*, in The Library of America series; it runs to over one thousand pages.

An earlier edition I relied on which includes a great many of his letters, and which is thoroughly indexed, was edited by Carl Van Doren: *Benjamin Franklin's Autobiographical Writings*, Viking, 1945. Such collections vary in their emphases according to the tastes and interests of their editors. I referred often to two of these: Kenneth Silverman, *Benjamin Franklin: The Autobiography and Other Writing*, Penguin, 1986, and Jessie L. Lemisch, *Benjamin Franklin: Autobiography and Other Writings*, Signet, 1961.

Almost all the quotations from Franklin in my book are taken from such primary sources.

Surprisingly, there have not been many modern lives of Franklin. Perhaps because Carl Van Doren's *Benjamin Franklin*, Viking, 1938, was so massive and detailed while at the same time so delightful that few ventured to rival him. But in the fifty years since Van Doren published, new research has unearthed material unknown to him. Esmond Wright has made excellent use of much of this in his *Franklin of Philadelphia*, Belknap, 1986. I owe much to both Van Doren and Wright.

Much earlier, within one year, two authors made useful surveys of Franklin's life under the headings of his richly varied activities. These were Paul L. Ford, *The Many-Sided Franklin*, Century, 1899, and Sidney George Fisher, *The True Benjamin Franklin*, Lippincott, 1899. The veteran biographer, Catherine Drinker Bowen, provides a beguiling portrait in her last book, *The Most Dangerous Man in America: Scenes from the Life of Benjamin Franklin*, Atlantic Monthly Press, 1974.

Many authors have examined Franklin's life from a single perspective. His scientific pursuits are explored in Ray Meador, *Franklin: Revolutionary Scientist*, University of Michigan, 1975, and in Bernard I. Cohen, *Franklin and Newton*, Harvard, 1956.

Concentrating on Franklin's earliest years, Arthur B. Tourtellot gives us invaluable details and insights in his *Benjamin Franklin: The Shaping of Genius, the Boston Years*, Doubleday, 1977. Useful material on early eighteenth-century apprentice-ship is found in W. J. Rorabaugh, *The Craft Apprentice: From Franklin to the Machine Age of America*, Oxford, 1986. For the role of printers and publishers in his day, I relied on Bernard Bailyn and J. B. Hench, *The Press and the American Revolution*, Northeastern University Press, 1986; James A. Suppenfield, *A Sweet Introduction: Franklin's Journalism as Literary Apprenticeship*, Southern Illinois University Press, 1973; and Benjamin Franklin V, *Boston Printers, Publishers and Booksellers*, G. K. Hall, 1980.

Special attention to Franklin's work as colonial agent in England is given in Cecil B. Currey, *Road to Revolution: Benjamin Franklin in England, 1765–1775*, Anchor, 1968. For his diplomatic service in France, there is Alred O. Aldridge, *Franklin and His French Contemporaries*, Greenwood, 1976, and Claude-Anne Lopez, *Mon Cher Papa: Franklin and the Ladies of Paris*, Yale, 1966.

The more intimate side of Franklin's family life is described in Claude-Anne Lopez and Eugenia W. Herbert, *The Private Franklin: The Man and His Family*, Norton, 1985, and in Willard Randall, *A Little Revenge: Benjamin Franklin and His Son*, Little, Brown, 1984.

Some scholars have collected essays on the many aspects of Franklin's life and work: as printer, publicist, traveler, autobiographer, almanac-maker, politician, diplomat. These can be found in J. A. Leo Lemay, *The Oldest Revolutionary: Essays on Ben-*

jamin Franklin, University of Pennsylvania, 1976; Roy N. Lokken, *Meet Dr. Franklin,* the Franklin Institute, 1981; and Esmond Wright, *Benjamin Franklin: A Profile,* Hill and Wang, 1968.

Living from 1706 to 1790, Franklin sweeps across the revolutionary century. There are scores of studies dealing with the America of his time, its economic and cultural life, the growth of the colonies, the Massachusetts and the Pennsylvania of his years, the events leading up to the Revolution, the political, diplomatic, and military aspects of the struggle for independence, and the shaping of the Constitution. Almost no such book is without reference to Franklin, whether for insights into what shaped him or into how he in turn influenced events.

A final word on the passages quoted from Franklin's writings. I have modernized them as to spelling, capitalization, punctuation, and paragraphing. This, only to make Franklin more easily accessible to today's readers, in preference to preserving the eighteenth-century modes.

INDEX

ABOUT THE AUTHOR

Milton Meltzer, distinguished biographer and historian, is the author of more than seventy books for young people and adults. Born in Worcester, Massachusetts, and educated at Columbia, he worked for the WPA Federal Theatre Project and then served in the air force in World War II. He has written for newspapers, magazines, radio and films, and has edited books, newspapers, and magazines.

The many honors for his books include five nominations for the National Book Award, and the Christopher, Jane Addams, Carter G. Woodson, Jefferson Cup, Washington Book Guild, Olive Branch, and Golden Kite awards. *Benjamin Franklin* is the latest of sixteen biographies, including such subjects as George Washington, Mark Twain, Langston Hughes, Dorothea Lange, Mary McLeod Bethune, and Winnie Mandela. One of his most recent books is a personal memoir, *Starting from Home: A Writer's Beginnings*.

Mr. Meltzer and his wife, Hildy, live in New York. They have two daughters, Jane and Amy, and a grandson, Benjamin. Meltzer is a member of the Author's Guild.